AND THE BEAT GOES ON
Towards A Sustainable Beloved Community

By Kevin A. Brown

And The Beat Goes On: Towards A Sustainable Beloved Community

ISBN 13: 979-8-218-12978-1

Cover Design: Miles Robinson of CIR-Design
Interior Design: Brandi K. Etheredge
Copyeditor: Yvette R. Blair

"It is profoundly important to turn our attention to "renewing a sense of beloved community." This is both the essence and the significance of Dr. Brown's book and we should heed his call. Building community at every level is the path towards a healthy and sustainable society that survives the destructiveness around us. Reverend Brown articulates crucial values for community development, shares our many success stories, and provides pathways for revitalization without displacement. What we need now is the political will."

Teresa Córdova, Ph.D
Director of the Great Cities Institute and Professor of Urban Planning and Policy at the University of Illinois at Chicago

"Kevin injects his values, his pragmatism, his lived experiences, and his unique skill sets of balancing strategic thinking and tactical abilities into a community development thesis that should be read and understood as a tour de force for progress."

Roy Alston
Founder, Tempo Novus
Community Economic Development Practitioner

"Dr. Kevin A. Brown uses this platform to demonstrate the true mission of universal Christianity as presented by Jesus that showcases the impartiality of Christ with no respect of person, the notion of universal humanity and brotherhood, unconditional love, and considers the needs of the least of these. Brown declares that we are the church and are commissioned to preach Christ's good news to everyone, empowering them through the Holy Spirit and has given new meaning to opening the doors of the church. In this, he has constructed a context where a church without walls utilizes the doctrine of Jesus to produce critical knowledge that will consequently enable us to become critical Christians—allowing for the church to construct relationships between our personal walk with God, community experiences, and public policy.

Maurice Hobson, Ph.D.
Historian, social scientist, Africana studies scholar, producer, and social justice champion based in Atlanta, Georgia

"In a perfect world, poverty and homelessness do not exist. In Dr. Kevin Brown's beloved community, as sketched in *And The Beat Goes On*, we are given hope for a tomorrow that includes love, justice, land, and wealth for all. Every library, community center, and faith builder needs this book as a brick and bridge for empowerment and action."

Janet Walsh, Ed.D.
Librarian

I thank my wife Shannon, and my children, Amiah and Kohen, for being my greatest gifts. I thank my parents, Larry and Rochelle, for the gift of life, and my entire family. Last but not least, my thanks go to my Beloved Community. You know who you are!

TABLE OF CONTENTS

Foreword 9

Preface 11

Introduction 13

Primer: Historical Context of Systemic Poverty
and Gentrification 19

Chapter 1: The Progressive Era 21

Chapter 2: The New Deal 23

Chapter 3: The Great Society 25

Chapter 4: The Working Poor 33

Chapter 5: Understanding Gentrification 37

Chapter 6: Poverty in the Bible 41

Chapter 7: Rethinking Our Theology to Help the Poor 51

Chapter 8: The Housing Crisis 63

Chapter 9: Empowerment 69

Chapter 10: Building a Community 77

Chapter 11: Martin Luther King, Jr. on Abolishing Poverty 87

Chapter 12: Factors Contributing to Poverty 99

Chapter 13: Where We Are Today 105

Chapter 14: What's Next 107

Chapter 15: What We Can Do to Create 6 Million Jobs
and 1.4 Million Businesses 113

Conclusion 121

Bibliography 125

FOREWORD

Rev. Dr. Kevin Brown has written holistically about raising the quality of life for all, for the United States and the world. In this well-researched work, he has made me realize that throughout my eighty-seven years, starting from when I was five, and getting involved in movements with Malcolm X, I have not seen the Beloved Community through such a lens.

This book opens our eyes to what we are missing and how we must approach the so-called Beloved Community. These pieces are relevant to us all. The United States has never meant for us to have this depth of analysis because of our so-called democracy. So if we are going to make America what it claims to be from the standpoint of democracy, it has to be with the approach of the information that Dr. Brown has provided.

Here is an opportunity for those who have been part of the civil and human rights movement to take the knowledge provided in this book, along with our own experiences, and fill in the missing pieces.

The Beloved Community, like the previous movements, included all people, irrespective of what their knowledge was, or whatever else, but simply because of what victimized us and what we aspired to become. *And The Beat Goes On* explains that and everything else.

This critical work gives us the information we need to develop our next generation with all the essential tools to make this nation what it long should have been. This book must be read and used to raise the quality of life, how it was meant to be, and how God's people have to be involved.

It is crucial because so much of the work practiced by the U.S. government and many non-profits and people perpetuates the status quo and implements more derogatory existences. Neighborhoods are in worse shape now than before they got involved. We have raised the quality of life. Pulling together all the elements of what Dr. Brown shows us gives us the capacity to become the Beloved Community, which includes increasing the quality of life so that everyone is rising.

For the world I hope to see, the Beloved Community is doable because we did it at Dudley Street to the degree possible under those circumstances. If we can do what we did without the research and information provided in this book, we can surely go past that now.

We have to create a design for what needs to follow for the greater good of trying to find this so-called democracy. We have food for the next generation when we arm politicians, students, activists, and everyday people with all the research and tools that are pulled together in this book. It shows the world a prototype of the Beloved Community. It takes love, analysis, and remembrance of things learned and the missing pieces.

Eugene "Gus" Newport, social justice activist
member of the *National Council of Elders*
and former *Director of the Dudley Street Neighborhood Initiative*

PREFACE

Our goal is to create a beloved community and this will require a qualitative change in our souls as well as a quantitative change in our lives."
Dr. Martin Luther King, Jr.

The title is inspired by civil rights leader, economist and humanitarian, Eugene "Gus" Newport, who has personally shared his wisdom with me and illuminated my path in this work. You will read more about him in chapters ten and fourteen and see the impact that he has on my work.

I wrote this book in the midst of the COVID-19 Pandemic. This is pandemic work, and it is for anyone who is curious enough and desires to know the truth of why poverty still exists in America, who is most affected, and more importantly, how we can work collectively to abolish it.

It is time for us to have a serious conversation about poverty. A modern approach must work to solve the current problem. Local- and state-level initiatives have the power to achieve a strategic approach to the Beloved Community. To truly accomplish a Beloved Community, the United States must abolish poverty.

When we adhere to what Dr. King prescribed in his work in 1967, poverty can be repealed in the same fashion that laws and states abolished slavery. A constitutional amendment that affirms there will be no poverty guarantees the absence of poverty. With an Economic

Bill of Rights alongside the existing Political Bill of Rights, economic rights will be protected. Fellow inhabitants of the United States, let us use this work to start a conversation about making the necessary changes.

Kevin A. Brown

INTRODUCTION

Mirror Mirror!

"One of the great liabilities of history is that all too many people fail to remain awake through great periods of social change. Every society has its protectors of the status quo and fraternities of the indifferent who are notorious for sleeping through revolutions. But today, our very survival depends on our ability to stay awake, to adjust to new ideas, to remain vigilant, and to face the challenge of change."

Dr. Martin Luther King, Jr.,
Where Do We Go From Here: Chaos or Community

It is hard to read the statement above and not think that it must have been written a few months ago or in the last year. These words written almost sixty years ago speak with glaring specificity to the status of where we find ourselves today. As a public theologian, activist, prophet, and preacher within the Black preaching tradition, King never failed to highlight the ills/evils (racism, militarism and materialism) that plague the soul of this nation. He also sought to offer thoughtful, insightful, and hope-filled actions and words born out of a tradition of people gifted with a righteous resilience that refused to accept things just as they are. He aimed his quest to build a more humane, just, and equitable society for all those made in the image of God. However, King and others (among them Fannie Lou Hamer, Ida B Wells, and Howard Thurman) were aware that this quest for the community must always situate the horrors and hopes of history in their proper context.

Many will ignore, distort, discount, or seek to destroy that truth when it paints a broader picture that does not embellish the narratives or myths many have come to accept as truth.

History forces us to look in the mirror. While the mirror serves as an instrument for correcting what is wrong or amiss, it also serves as a reminder that things have and are changing before our eyes. The changes we have experienced since March 2020 with the onset of the global coronavirus (COVID-19) pandemic have forced us to wake up, adjust, and remain vigilant in facing the unrelenting winds of change. Over the past two years, collectively as a nation and individually, we have had to spend more time in front of the mirror (actually and metaphorically) than many of us would like.

These past two years have forced us to look in the mirror as we watched multiple incidents of infractions against humanity. George Floyd, Ahmaud Aubrey, Breonna Taylor, and many other Black Americans were not granted the same dignity as other Americans who encounter police, jog in the community, or sleep in bed. The mirror forced us to take more time and sit with *The New York Times 1619 Project*, initiated and curated by journalist Nikole Hannah-Jones, stirring a new dialogue about which United States' narratives are prioritized.

The mirror forced us to deal with a virus that continues to ravage people globally while also ravaging communities of color in the United States at a far greater pace than other communities – a deadly respiratory virus that should have been handled with seriousness, expediency, strategy, and compassion. Instead, the virus was handled with arrogance, criminal negligence, ignorance, and a lack of empathy for those suffering before and during the pandemic. The pandemic exposed the long history of neglect, insensitivity, and lack of compassion for those in impoverished communities and especially for people of color. As a result of the confluence of these events, some looked in the mirror and decided to do something about what they saw and did not like. Many responded through protests, writing books, running for office, returning to school, starting businesses, working on legislation, voting in record numbers, resigning from jobs, and camping out at state capitols. Many decided to do something to ensure that the current reflection of dehumanization and the myth of white supremacy would not endure. Their actions also served as a testament that they did not remain asleep through a great revolution.

One of those persons is the prophet and practical theologian, preacher, teacher, and community advocate, Dr. Kevin A. Brown. During the pandemic, Brown participated in serving communities dealing with the impact of COVID-19, Hurricane Ida, and power outages in Texas. Not only did Kevin assist communities with resources while leveraging community partnerships, he did not go to sleep during the revolution. He decided not to look away from the mirror but instead to gaze into the mirror long enough to offer a critical and creative reflection on the truth of what he saw there. These contributing factors helped create (in many instances) and sustain poverty, causing communities of color to be more susceptible to the deadly results experienced prior to and during the pandemic. Dr. Brown decided that during this time of disruption, he would look into the mirror and provide a historical analysis of public policy ranging from The New Deal, The War on Poverty, and The History of Gentrification. He also examined the chasm between federal legislation and local actualization. By starting with the history of public policy and the so-called systems put in place to address poverty, followed by insight concerning the language regarding the working poor, he then turns his attention to why that chasm has continued to grow over the last fifty years.

This work is timely as it offers a needed perspective concerning what lies at the root of this growing chasm which remains a constant threat to democracy and the possibility of sustainable and loving communities. It is a moral divide, not just a political or ideological divide. This moral divide highlighted by Dr. King previously and Rev. Dr. William Barber and Repairers of the Breach now, is often missing from the conversation. Public policy, job creation, capital access, and flourishing community models should always be prioritized. When morality is part of the conversation, it is usually talked about from the perspective of American civil religion, which prioritizes the flag, the gun, control over female bodies, and a distorted view of the Bible as justification for truncated or dangerous public policy.

In *And The Beat Goes On*, Kevin remains keenly aware—as King, Barber, and others are—that helpful legislation can be passed (or not). However, there also has to be a fundamental change in heart and mind coupled with an expansive theo-logical and theo-ethical lens and language. *Theo-Logic: the narratives and images that define how people talk and think about who is divine, the interpretation of the Bible, and the role of faith in public life. Theo-Ethic: how those definitions influence policies that determine what communities deserve dignity, resources, access, safety, and a chance for sustainability.* The text calls for a public policy that reflects a moral and ethical orientation that builds sustainable communities, while simultaneously inviting the reader to consider a broader theological outlook and lexicon that creates policies and practices that are more liberatory than lethal.

Throughout the text, Dr. Brown beckons us back to the mirror to look, listen, and consider Dr. King's words from *Where Do We Go From Here*. This text also considers what a vision for Sustainable

Beloved Community looks like within the United States. Although staring in the mirror can be a challenge, we are reminded in these pages to look ahead and get a glimpse of a vision that compels us to become active agents and architects redefining and developing sustainable communities together. This book offers the much needed and often overlooked problematic intersection of poverty, American Exceptionalism, and American Civil Religion which helps to create and justify why some have and others do not deserve to have. In the spirit of Sankofa, that is, a West African concept of looking back to fetch from the past what is useful for the present, Kevin responds to Dr. King's ever-hopeful disposition regarding our power to create a better world and use a new love language. Moreover, *And The Beat Goes On* offers a fresh approach to thinking and acting with a practical theology, and with a Christocentric focus that demands love, justice, and compassion for all.

Rev. Damien Durr, DCD Empowerment

And The Beat Goes On: Towards A Sustainable Beloved Community

A PRIMER ON HISTORICAL CONTEXT OF SYSTEMIC POVERTY AND GENTRIFICATION

Over the last 120 years, there have been three occasions in the United States when poverty was considered a significant public issue. These occasions are typically referred to as the Progressive Era, the New Deal, and the Great Society.

That is not to say that poverty did not exist before that time, but rather that before 1900, people thought poverty to be a problem only for the poor and not a public issue that affected us all.

In each of these three instances, urbanization and industrialization collided, producing great wealth as well as widespread urban poverty. This created a situation that made it nearly impossible to ignore the disproportion between the rich and the poor. In these instances, when efforts were raised to do something about poverty, wars diverted attention. When the wars concluded, the nation's emphasis was on getting the country back to a state of normality. Unfortunately in the United States, normal meant that poverty was ignored as a public issue (Copeland 1994, 25).

CHAPTER 1
THE PROGRESSIVE ERA

Robert Hunter published a book in 1904 called *Poverty*; some scholars might credit him with revealing poverty as a public issue. In that book, he explored three main issues: the differences between dependency and poverty, the idea that poverty was much more widespread than initially thought, and the idea that most of the poor (not the dependent) were poor due to social forces rather than personal failings. Also present during this time period were ten settlement houses and the Charity Organization Society. These two groups were composed mainly of middle-class citizens, characterized by their "thirst for open inquiry and a drive for action" (Copeland 1994, 29). Both groups recognized the importance of relationship-building between the poor and non-poor and advocated for self-help over random almsgiving. The settlement-house organization was also interested in a two-way learning relationship with the poor. Both groups believed in a system of scientific inquiry to identify the causes of pauperism, discovering both social and personal causes.

One of the most critical findings of the settlement-house workers was "that what distinguished the rich from the poor was not personal character so much as social situation" (30). Each settlement house was located within the community of the poor, allowing the settlement-house workers to build identities as a part of the poor neighborhood. The settlement houses became part of the community, focusing on community association and integrity instead of charity, while the Charity Organization Society visitors considered it their responsibility to provide an incentive for the poor to rise above poverty. The settlement house movement showed a commitment to democratic politics, including the belief that the poor had opinions that carried equal weight to those of the wealthy. This belief manifested itself in the form of open forums where ideas and opinions could be shared, resulting in the development of common purposes and actions. Settlement-house workers were able to use the data and statistics they collected to make their case that the social problems faced by the urban poor were political issues that needed to be addressed by a democratic society (Copeland 1994, 31).

CHAPTER 2
THE NEW DEAL

In the midst of and following the Great Depression, it was inevitable that unemployment would become a public issue. Some characteristics of the New Deal that set it apart from earlier reform efforts were the realities of the Great Depression. Unemployment was not reserved for the minority; instead, the majority of Americans feared that they were on the brink of becoming poor during the Great Depression. The economic system did not seem to be working effectively for anyone. The problem was not confined to the local or state level but reached much broader to the national level.

In the trenches of the Great Depression, there was a consensus that something had to be done. When President Franklin D. Roosevelt took office in 1932, it was with a promise to do *something*, but not a clear plan as to what that *something* would be. The result is what is now referred to as the New Deal. There were two phases to the New Deal: the National Recovery Administration and the Keynesian fiscal policy. Both phases had the main goal of economic recovery, with the afterthought of dealing with poverty (Copeland 1994, 34). Keynesian is derived from John Maynard Keynes, a British economist, who in the 1930s theorized that consumer demand is the primary driving force in an economy. This theory suggests that government should allocate funding on things like unemployment benefits, infrastructure, and education. In other words, it should be a policy (Nelson 2006, 2).

Harry Hopkins is thought to have had the most influence over policy and understanding of poverty during this time, as evidenced by authorizing spending of $8.5 trillion aimed at unemployment relief for fifteen million Americans. Hopkins, who served as adviser to President Roosevelt, administrator of the Federal Emergency Relief Administration, and later as Secretary of Commerce, aligned himself with two major principles (Copeland 1994, 35): that the dignity of the poor and unemployed should be respected and supported, and that the government had a responsibility to the poor and unemployed. These principles were directly aligned with the views stated by Roosevelt, but Hopkins was able to articulate them more concretely: "Above all else, the New Deal stressed that in a democracy the government must be responsive to the needs of its citizens" (36).

Unfortunately, not much had changed in the fact that those in power did not actually represent the poor, but merely served the interests of the poor. Like many efforts before it, the New Deal aimed to provide economic recovery in general and not specifically to eliminate poverty. The New Deal was unable to reorganize the economy or provide a significant redistribution of wealth. When war once again entered American reality, it diverted attention away from the issue of poverty and stimulated the economy, leading to less of the widespread unemployment which had reinforced the justification for the aid of the poor. The end of the Second World War left America once again desiring to return to a state of normal. The remnants of the New Deal were seen in the Employment Act of 1946 and in the staff of the various government agencies dealing with the poor (Copeland 1994, 39).

CHAPTER 3
THE GREAT SOCIETY

During the 1960s, poverty was somewhat "re-discovered." Most Americans were not poor, and they assumed that most others were not either, and that if they were poor, it was by choice.

On the local level, civil rights organizations became more public, making the recognition of urban decay more apparent. By the 1960s, it became clear that while urban renewal brought new buildings, enterprises, and people, it did little to solve the old problems. President John F. Kennedy was looking for ways to respond to the civil rights movement that was gaining momentum. His goal was to respond in such a way that was not completely uncompromising to the poor, working-class white citizens. He desired to begin a domestic program similar to the international program, the Peace Corps. He hoped that such a program would later enable his administration to be viewed in a good moral light. Kennedy's speechwriter, Theodore Sorensen, introduced the president to Dwight Macdonald's work on poverty. From there, Kennedy's top economic advisor, Walter Heller, was instructed to draft plans for a War on Poverty. In March of 1964, following the assassination of Kennedy, President Lyndon B. Johnson was introduced to this idea and proposed a War on Poverty, saying that while the country often had cause to assert war against foreign enemies, the time had come for the country to declare war on a domestic enemy that was threatening the well-being and strength of the country's own people (Copeland 1994, 39). The domestic enemy, which was poverty, was unknown to a majority of Americans. The War on Poverty was fueled by growing factors on both the local and national level.

On the national level, urban renewal was intended to assist in the war but instead ended up rearranging the existing problems (Copeland 1994, 40) .

An estimated 1,600 Black neighborhoods were destroyed by urban renewal. The devastation was twofold. On the one hand, residents saw their world—their immediate neighborhood—fall apart around them. On the other hand, the entire population of Black America was shaken due to their extreme interconnectedness. This devastation dealt a crushing blow to the community's ability to function, which in turn left the Black world at a disadvantage when it came to their ability to meet the demands of globalization (Fullilove, Peterson, and Bassett 2016, 19 Kindle).

Urban renewal is a term generally used to describe improvements in cities. In the United States, it also refers to government programs that began under the Housing Act of 1949. The programs were modified numerous times, and under the Housing Act of 1954, the term was finally introduced into law. The term has come to be used as a synonym for progress. The Housing Acts were designed to provide money needed to shift the economic focus following the Second World War. "Marc Weiss summed up the overall impact of the twenty-four-year program by saying, 'Urban renewal agencies in many cities demolished whole communities inhabited by low-income people in order to provide land for private development of office buildings, sports arenas, hotels, trade centers, and high-income luxury buildings. Rather than providing decent homes and suitable living environments, urban renewal created a massive housing crisis'" (Fullilove, Peterson, and Bassett 2016, 58 Kindle). The number of public housing units built at the sites was severely disproportionate to the number of residential units that were destroyed. There was a need to reorganize cities in order to meet the changing needs of American entrepreneurship. Powerful and wealthy men were the primary backers for this change and they pushed for their solutions to become law—because it would benefit them. Urban renewal is a result of those men's interest in the property and businesses in the central part of cities. Fullilove states that part of the discourse on the changing city was the African American community's sense of threat, which was captured in the expression "Urban Renewal is Negro Removal" (Fullilove, Peterson, and Bassett 2016, 61 Kindle).

The poor were displaced into new areas or concentrated in large public housing complexes (Copeland 1994, 40). Lloyd Ohlin and Richard Cloward are notable figures of this era, committed to fighting poverty through community action. One of their most notable projects was a study of juvenile delinquency, in which they "argued that delinquency was primarily caused not by problems with the individuals or the groups to which they belonged but by broader social forces" (Copeland 1994, 41). They showed that while youth were able to observe the values of the cultures around them, they did not have the means necessary to bring those values into their realities, so delinquency was their chosen alternative. The authors took it even further, explaining that the effort of those wishing to eliminate delinquency should strive to reorganize the slum communities. These ideas were new and aligned with the concerns of those that believed that urban problems should be dealt with politically.

The organization, Mobilization for Youth, also contributed to the reform movement of this time period. The two main objectives of this organization were social change and doing something to change the realization that established institutions like schools, hospitals, government and political organizations represented their own personal interests rather than the interests of the community as a whole (Copeland 1994, 43). Central to what Mobilization for Youth wanted most was to place control in the hands of the people living in the low-income neighborhoods instead of in the hands of outsiders. They believed in a theory that said people act out of self-interest, and that therefore politicians could not be expected to help solve the problems of the urban slums without the motivation of having something to gain from their actions. As Copeland (1994) explains, "Mobilization for Youth merged a social theory about the causes of delinquency with a political theory about the motivation of human action" (43).

Although the War on Poverty set the political tone for this era, most of its efforts seemed to revert to the old ways and beliefs of stressing education and training as the primary ways to assist individuals in getting out of poverty. There were few programs that intentionally created jobs. Still, it became apparent that "education and job training are of little long-range consequence in abolishing poverty unless coupled with full employment" (Copeland 1994, 45). As in previous time periods, the war in Vietnam diverted Americans' time, attention, and money away from the issue of poverty. After Richard Nixon was elected as the new president, the Great Society decelerated as did its efforts to liberate the country of poverty. Instead of the new administration looking for ways to redistribute the nation's wealth, the poor were ignored. Inadequate nourishment, medical services, education, and housing left them segregated from and unqualified to compete in broader society (McKissick 1969, 24).

Because poverty was not a prominent topic in public discourse, the climate was ripe not only for gentrification but for other racial disparities as well. I don't intend to exclude any group or race; rather, to see poverty through the lens of African Americans gives us an example of how the United States system socially engineered what is now known as systemic poverty and gentrification: "White America has refused to accept its responsibilities to the black poor—the product of brutal slavery, blocked every step of the way from participating in the economy, prevented even from being 'homesteaders,' left landless, moneyless, and uneducated after the civil war. At no time did America offer an opportunity to the black masses; at no time did the black population receive chances offered by every other group of immigrants" (McKissick 1969, 24).

In the United States of America, the color of one's skin is used as a visible tool of persecution and a way to enforce financial constraints. Color defines caste, and class defines economic status (McKissick 1969, 24). In *The Souls of Black Folk*, W.E.B. Du Bois argued that the problem of the twentieth century is the problem of the color line. His argument is unfortunately all too relevant today.

The fact that Black people have been brutally and systematically underdeveloped in America's economic history is obvious. The existence of Black people (or another underclass) is necessary in order to perpetuate and maintain an imbalance of the economic system that systematically disenfranchises Black Americans – a system to which we have grown accustomed. As Manning Marable, who was a political scientist, scholar, and professor of African American studies (1983) argues, "The relationship is filled with paradoxes: each advance in white freedom was purchased by black enslavement; white affluence coexists with black poverty; white state and corporate is the product in part of black powerlessness; income mobility for the few is rooted in income stasis for the many" (1). Blacks are discounted through racial discrimination, which leads to them being underemployed and politically marginalized.

A different opinion on this issue is that because Blacks have been integrated so well into the system, they inhabit the lowest rung on the ladder of American socioeconomic upward progress. The United States' democratically elected government deliberately maximizes Black oppression. For the manipulation of Blacks as both consumers and workers bolsters capitalist development. Black Americans have never been equal partners in the American Social Contract, because the system exists not to develop, but to under-develop Black people (Marable 1983, 1). Marable also asserts, "Underdevelopment was the direct consequence of this process: chattel slavery, sharecropping, peonage, industrial labor at low wages, and cultural chaos. The current economic amnesia of the West is therefore no accident, because it reveals the roots of massive exploitation and human degradation upon which the current world order rests" (5–6).

The inalienable rights of African Americans were not protected at the Constitutional Convention of 1787, where the U.S. Constitution was drafted, adopted and ratified. The main concerns for those in charge included guaranteeing property rights, with property including other humans, principally through slavery. This resulted in a racist declaration that protected the institution by strategically omitting the words "slave" or "slavery" (Marable 1983, 4). At the center of every issue relating to power, culture, society, and economic production was and is racism. According to W. E. B. Du Bois, justice for the American Negro was the primary obstacle to American democracy (13). Du Bois also asserts that racism was a major problem for more than just nonwhites. The needs of oppressed people could not and would not be met until antiracist politics were established. (13)

In the first half of the twentieth century, governments, both local and federal, created mortgage programs that discriminated against and prevented minority populations from homeownership. They also embedded restrictive conditions within property deeds that prohibited property ownership of certain properties by certain races. This action paved the way for white populations to gain access to certain resources necessary for homeownership, contributing to racial segregation in American cities ("Mapping the Legacy of Structural Racism in Philadelphia," n.d.).

During the 1930s, discriminatory lending practices became commonplace at the federal level when the Home Owners' Loan Corporation and the Federal Housing Administration were created. Following the Great Depression, programs like these provided financial support to homeowners, with the goal of increasing homeownership. The Federal Housing Administration provided federal insurance for mortgages and relied on neighborhood appraisals created by the Home Owners' Loan Corporation in order to limit or restrict insurance for individuals from neighborhoods deemed "risky." Unfortunately, the appraisals included an explicit racial component ("Mapping the Legacy of Structural Racism in Philadelphia," n.d.). These discriminatory practices were a causative factor in driving lending services into the private sector, creating more barriers for African Americans and encouraging white populations to move into neighborhoods that were becoming increasingly racially uniform. The definition of "white" broadened to include many other populations, all the while causing massive drops in property values in neighborhoods that were primarily African American. Eventually, the homeownership programs through the 1960s permitted wealth accumulation for certain populations while overtly preventing African Americans from partaking in accruing wealth ("Mapping the Legacy of Structural Racism in Philadelphia," n.d.).

While discriminatory housing policies, as well as redlining, were made illegal in 1968 with the passing of the Fair Housing Act and the Civil Rights Act, to this day discriminatory lending persists in the form of reverse redlining. In this practice, mortgage lenders charge higher interest rates and lenders' fees for African Americans and Latinos, in comparison with their white equivalents. There have been numerous class-action lawsuits against mortgage lenders because of this in the years since the Great Recession ("Mapping the Legacy of Structural Racism in Philadelphia," n.d.).

Areas that have been historically redlined in urban cities continue to experience higher amounts of poverty, unemployment, and violent crime, as well as limited educational access and poor health outcomes compared to other neighborhoods in the city. Lacking access to equitable lending and legal deed ownership, minority populations are forced to inhabit neighborhoods that the federal government considers unworthy of its investment. Nearly a century later, the result is segregated neighborhoods that are denied basic opportunities to equalize outcomes ("Mapping the Legacy of Structural Racism in Philadelphia," n.d.).

CHAPTER 4

THE WORKING POOR

In America, poverty does not discriminate based on race or ethnicity. Although African Americans often attend inferior schools, live in run-down neighborhoods, and battle racial discrimination on a daily basis, poverty also extends universal hardships to people of all races. White Americans who make up the bottom of the working world struggle to overcome many of the same obstacles that obstruct Blacks. However, still living under the shadow of slavery, Blacks remain overrepresented among low-income Americans and face many discriminations that poor white people do not (Shipler 2009, 103 Kindle).

Lyndon B. Johnson's War on Poverty never truly mobilized the country, nor was it pursued to victory (Shipler 2009, 6 Kindle). Fifty years later, after all our economic achievements, the gap between the rich and the poor has only widened, with a median net worth of $1,589,900 among the top 10 percent and negative $4,900 for the bottom 25 percent, meaning that they owe more than they own (Shipler 2009, 6 Kindle).

Finding one's identity within poverty is a struggle that has helped to shape the debate about social policies, including welfare. The poor have less protection from the government, less freedom to circumvent the obstacles that arise from living in a competition-driven world, and less control over their own decisions in general (Shipler 2009, 7 Kindle). In fact, "Poverty, then, does not lend itself to an easy definition" (Shipler 2009, 7 Kindle). Shipler states, "It may be absolute, an inability to buy basic necessities. It may be relative, an inability to buy the lifestyle that prevails at a certain time and place. It cannot be measured by a universal yardstick or by an index of disparity. Even dictionaries cannot agree" (7 Kindle).

The economic expansion of the 1990s resulted in rising incomes which led to a decline in official poverty. The new decade saw a poverty rate fall from 15.1 percent to 11.3 percent by 1993. It then rose slightly to 12.5 percent in 2003, 12.3 percent in 2006, and to 15.2 percent in 2011. These figures, however, are misleading. The formula used to determine the poverty level was designed in 1964, leaving the poverty line well below the amount that is needed in the present-day to sustain a decent living. Slight revisions to the formula in the years following adjust for inflation but fail to take into account the lifestyle changes that occurred in the corresponding half-century (Shipler 2009, 9 Kindle).

We are left with a distorted reality of the number of people who in reality could be considered to be living in poverty. The Census Bureau and the National Academy of Sciences have tested formulas that seem to be more accurate as they take into account actual costs of expenses like food, clothing, shelter, and utilities. The calculations would include any types of government assistance as income, and cost of living calculations would include child care, doctor's expenses, and health insurance. In 1998, when various formulas were run, the proportion of the population in poverty went up from 34.5 million to 42.2 million and the supplemental Poverty Measure which was introduced in 2011, saw a poverty rate increase from 15.2 to 16 percent" (Shipler 2009, 10 Kindle).

For families living in poverty, there are many factors. Financial, psychological, personal, societal, past and present factors all contribute to the situation, and all of these are intertwined, creating a domino effect: "A run-down apartment can exacerbate a child's asthma, which leads to a call for an ambulance, which generates a medical bill that cannot be paid, which ruins a credit record, which hikes the interest rate on an auto loan, which forces the purchase of an unreliable used car, which jeopardizes a mother's punctuality at work, which limits her promotions and earning capacity, which confines her to poor housing" (Shipler 2009, 10 Kindle).

It stands to reason, then, that if there is not a single, stand-alone cause, there is also not a single, stand-alone solution. Fixing one piece of the puzzle is not enough if all of the pieces are not adequately addressed. We must not only recognize the problems, but also recognize the people. All too often people go to work every day but remain in poverty. These are the people that are so easily overlooked as they blend into the society around us. Nobody who works hard should be poor in America (Shipler 2009, 11 Kindle).

CHAPTER 5

UNDERSTANDING GENTRIFICATION

Gentrification occurs when higher-income residents of a different race move into a neighborhood that has been historically disinvested, bringing with them economic change. There is a demographic shift marked by a change in the income level as well as the educational level of the residents. Gentrification is a complex process and in order to fully understand it, one must consider the historic conditions that left the community vulnerable to gentrification, the impact gentrification has on communities, and the way that the historic conditions of the community impact the city investment patterns ("Gentrification Explained | Urban Displacement Project" 2017).

Historic Conditions

From the 1930s through the 1960s, the federal government set standards that labeled neighborhoods composed mostly of people of color as "risky" and "unfit for investment." These standards were conveyed through the banks, making it difficult for people of color to access loans that would allow them to buy or repair homes in their neighborhoods. This practice was known as redlining ("Gentrification Explained | Urban Displacement Project" 2017).

White Flight

"White Flight" refers to a time in the mid-twentieth century where housing and transportation policies fueled the growth of white suburbs, driving money out of urban centers. The GI Bill was one of these programs. It made low-cost mortgage loans available for soldiers returning from World War II.

However, the extent to which Black veterans were able to purchase homes in the growing suburbs was severely limited by discrimination. "In fact, the FHA largely required that suburban developers agreed to not sell houses to black people in order for developers to access these guaranteed loans" ("Gentrification Explained | Urban Displacement Project" 2017).

Foreclosure Crisis

More recently, communities have become more vulnerable to gentrification due to the foreclosure crisis. With unbalanced levels of subprime lending resulting in mass foreclosures, these low-income communities of color have been left vulnerable to investors whose aim is to purchase and flip homes for profit. "Of foreclosures completed in 2007-2009, there were: 790 foreclosures for African Americans, 769 foreclosures for Latinos, and 452 non-Hispanic Whites per 10,000 loans" ("Gentrification Explained | Urban Displacement Project" 2017).

City Disinvestment and Investment Patterns

Today, both people and money are flowing back into these historically disinvested neighborhoods for a number of reasons. The rental market is getting more expensive, and residents are looking for lower housing costs. Older, historic houses have a certain appeal to new residents, and these neighborhoods tend to be in close proximity to jobs and restaurants in city centers. In an effort to draw new residents, cities are investing in improving the infrastructure and transit access ("Gentrification Explained | Urban Displacement Project" 2017).

Signs of Gentrification

To the citizens, gentrification may look like investors buying, rehabbing, and selling properties for large profits, an increase in investment in neighborhood amenities, a shift in land use, and changes in businesses as they shift to cater to the needs of the new residents ("Gentrification Explained | Urban Displacement Project" 2017).

The Impact of Gentrification

Although one positive aspect of gentrification is an increase of investment in an area, a major downside is the displacement of long-term residents that are unable to stay and partake in the benefits of the new housing and public transportation. Cultural displacement is also an issue in these areas. For those that are able to stay in the neighborhood, changes in the cultural makeup and character of the neighborhood can lead to a sense of feeling out of place in their own neighborhood. When a neighborhood is gentrified, middle-class people move into a disinvested neighborhood, exerting economic, political, and social pressures upon the existing community. When you remove people that have built the neighborhood, you remove the soul and DNA of a community ("Impacts of Gentrification: A Policy Primer" 2016).

Gentrification has other downfalls. In many cases, the poor citizens become displaced, and businesses that are unique to the neighborhood are replaced by wealthier businesses. The influx of wealthier and higher-skilled citizens, as well as larger corporations, brings a higher cost of living which often pushes out the low-income residents. Unable to compete for the housing that they cannot afford, they are often forced into poorer neighborhoods that they can afford. ("Impacts of Gentrification: A Policy Primer" 2016).

When previously poor neighborhoods see an increase of wealthier residents, the median income of the area rises. This creates a larger cash flow for the local businesses, which in turn makes it more desirable for people to invest in local businesses. As time goes on, more businesses mean more jobs and higher wages.

There also may be benefits of gentrification that extend beyond the private sector. As wealthier residents contribute more income tax to city reserves and more expensive homes lead to higher property taxes, the local government receives increased tax revenues. This increased revenue allows the local government to spend more on public transportation, infrastructure, public schools, and other services that benefit the citizens.

CHAPTER 6

POVERTY IN THE BIBLE

The study of poverty and its historical relevance and connection to biblical times needs to focus on the abolition of poverty rather than the temporary taming of it. The abolition of poverty must be considered in correlation with the biblical messages and interpretations of those messages in order to develop a practical plan of action: "Reflection on poverty should be a constant part of the theological discourse to prevent theology from becoming a mental exercise that is distant from the realities and suffering of this world" (Scheffler 2013, 12).

Brief History of Biblical Poverty

Poverty was a problem in ancient Israel just as it is today. There are multiple terms used to describe poverty throughout the Bible, which means that multiple meanings can be attached to the term "poor." In the Hebrew Bible, the terms for poverty usually refer to material poverty, however they could also range from "the worst kind of destitution to any kind of misery or suffering, including suffering at the spiritual level" (Scheffler 2013, 4). Poverty is most often viewed in its most basic form, material destitution. Compared to other issues examined or mentioned in the Bible, the references to poverty are small in number. This may be attributed to the fact that the people who wrote the Bible were not the people who were experiencing poverty. The people who were affected by poverty were more consumed with surviving than with reflecting on their current situations and were most likely unable to read or write. It is because of this that it is significant that there are references to the poor at all (Scheffler 2013, 7).

The Old Testament uses several terms to describe poverty:

ani/anw – poor and humble

ebjon – socially weak, miserable, poor

dal – low, helpless, insignificant, poor

rasj – usually refers to material poverty (Scheffler 2013, 7)

In the Old Testament, particularly in Exodus, Leviticus and Deuteronomy, it is advised that the poor be treated kindly (Scheffler 2013, 7). In the Deuteronomic history, a history of Israel is presented that brings to light Israel's failures and calls for the implementation of a positive attitude towards the poor. This is most clearly exemplified in Hannah's song in 1 Samuel 2:1-10 and the story of Naboth's vineyard in 1 Kings 21:1-9. (Scheffler 2013, 7)

In Nehemiah 5, the story is told of a ruler who sacrifices his rights to remedy the country's poverty. In the midst of the economic crisis that was happening in Jerusalem, people took to the streets to decry their condition and lodge their complaints against the government. It was akin to a modern-day protest. The powers that be in Judah had little to no regard for the well-being of its citizens; thus, Nehemiah called out the injustice of swelling debt and admonished the ruling powers for being complicit in the situation that led to the majority of the people being in poverty.

Meanwhile, the New Testament uses different terms to describe poverty:

Ptochos – poverty in its most literal sense, people who are poor and highly destitute to the point of begging

Penes – refers to a person who is poor, must live sparingly, and can merely survive, not as severe as ptochos

Endess – similar to ptochos, with emphasis on a more severe lack of resources rather than a continuous state of poverty

Penichros – same as ptochos (Scheffler 2013, 7)

"In the New Testament the emphasis on poverty can be traced back to the historical Jesus who, according to the oldest witnesses, was poor himself (Lk 9:58), but pronounced the poor blessed (Lk 6:20–21; Mt 5:3), preached for them (Lk 7:22), cared for them through the multiplication of the bread and gave his disciples the responsibility of caring for them (Mk 6:37; Lk 12:33; Mk 10:21; Lk 16:19-31)" (Scheffler 2013, 8). The Gospels reflect numerous times of Jesus caring for the poor. Luke and Acts are the writings that most significantly deal with the issue of poverty. In the New Testament, we see the interrelated issues of physical and mental illness, social ostracization, and human suffering as they relate to poverty. In the New Testament texts, the goal is always to abolish poverty, especially severe poverty (Scheffler 2013, 8).

Why did Jesus Come to Earth?

When the question, "Why did Jesus come to Earth?" is asked among the faith community, the most common answer usually has something to do with dying on the cross to save us from our sins, so we can go to heaven. While this explanation carries truth, Jesus' message was much broader and more profound than that. In Col. 1:15-20, "Jesus Christ is described as the Creator, Sustainer, and Reconciler of *everything*. Yes, Jesus died for our sins, but He also died to reconcile – that is, to put into the right relationship – all that He created" (Corbett 2014, 33). If that was Jesus' mission, then it is only logical that the task of the Church, the task of God's people, should be fully aligned with that mission. Jesus spread his mission through both his words and his actions; thus God's Church and God's people are called to do the same.

Jesus as an Interpretation

According to Howard Washington Thurman, theologian, scholar, and civil rights leader who also served as a Morehouse College professor, there are a few simple facts that must be considered when looking at Jesus in relation to poverty. First, Jesus was a Jew. Second, Jesus was a poor Jew. Third, "Jesus was a member of a minority group in the midst of a larger dominant and controlling group" (Thurman 1996, 18). When taking these factors into consideration, it must also be asked: why, when there were many others facing the same conditions, was Jesus set apart from all of the others? In Jesus' time, the political and social climate in Israel was volatile. Yet it was then that Jesus began his teaching and his ministry: "His message focused on the urgency of a radical change in the inner attitude of the people. He recognized fully that out of the heart are the issues of life and that no external force, however great and overwhelming, can at long last destroy a people if it does not first win the victory of the spirit against them" (Thurman 1996, 21).

There are a limited number of explanations that break down what Jesus' life and his teachings say to those individuals in the exact moment in time when they find themselves in a seemingly hopeless situation. (Thurman 1996, 11) Those individuals searching for relief and support – assistance to get through their daily lives with some semblance of self-respect – have often found Christianity to be im-personal and unbeneficial. The orthodox Christian word is unclear and unspecific. It has become far too commonplace that in order to feel secure and respected by society, people practicing Christianity align themselves with a model of strong against weak: "This is a matter of tremendous significance, for it reveals to what extent religion that was born of a people acquainted with persecution and suffering has become the cornerstone of a civilization and of nations whose very position in modern life has too often been secured by a ruthless use of power applied to weak and defenseless peoples" (Thurman 1996, 12).

There is something about tending to the needs of others out of one's own abundant supply that provides a sense of personal uplift. For this reason, our desire to serve as missionaries comes out of an obligation of Christians to assist the needy and those Thurman calls the "backward peoples of the earth" (1996, 12).

It is the natural instinct at the core of Christianity to take what one has found to be personally valuable and share it with others. With this instinct should also come a certain measure of caution, for it is very difficult to refrain from expressing some amount of condescension for individuals facing situations that naturally cry out for assistance (Thurman 1996, 12).

According to Thurman, possibly the greatest religious quest of modern life deals with the question of what our religion offers to those individuals who need their own needs met but also desire to provide assistance to others who may have greater needs. How does our religion attempt to meet their needs? Jesus was not afforded the regular sense of security that comes with belonging to the majority, nor was he able to partake in the general perks of citizenship because he was not a Roman citizen (Thurman 1996, 33). In fact, he had so few civil guarantees that he had to find other sources of general and overall comfort and well-being. The environment of the time was one wrought with uncertainty. While he had a firm grasp of the intentions of religion, he was also well aware that those intentions could never come to fruition within the current structure.

From the depths of that structure, he had visions of the needed comfort being available to all: "There would be room for all, and no man would be a threat to his brother. 'The Kingdom of God is within.' The Spirit of the Lord is upon me because he hath anointed me to preach the gospel to the poor" (Thurman 1996, 35).

Poverty According to the Gospels

Obery Hendricks, a scholar who is known for his work at the intersection of religion and the American political economy, observed in his book, *The Politics of Jesus: Rediscovering the True Revolutionary Nature of the Teachings of Jesus*, that the world reflected the Gospels in two distinct classes of the very rich, and the very poor. In Israel, the very rich represented up to a mere five percent of the total population. In this very rich class were the Roman bureaucrats, aristocratic priests, wealthy landowners, and successful tax collectors. The other 95 percent of the population were very poor, most so poor that they could be labeled destitute. In the rabbinic writings are depictions of clusters of homeless poor people wandering the countryside (Hendricks 2006, Kindle 1088). These people were so desperate for sustenance that when the poor tithe was distributed, the pandemonium that ensued resembled a wild animal stampede. In Matthew 20:1-16, note vv. 3-7, there is a recounting of gatherings of unemployed village workers so desperate for a day's wage that they would accept jobs without inquiring as to how much the pay would be. Hendricks states, the Gospel of Luke describes Mary "as giving thanks to God that among the acts of salvation set in motion by the Messiah she carried in her womb, would be filling the hungry 'with good things' (Luke 1:53)" (Hendricks 2006, Kindle 1088). The sad observation by a second-century rabbi that "the daughters of Israel are comely, but poverty makes them repulsive" could easily have been written with the Israel of Jesus' day in mind (Hendricks 2006, Kindle 1088).

Good News for the Poor

"The spirit of the Lord is upon me, because he has anointed me to bring good news to the poor. He has sent me to proclaim release to the captives and recovery of sight to the blind, to let the oppressed go free, to proclaim the year of the Lord's favor" (Luke 4:18-19, NRSV).

According to Wesley Bergen, the New Testament Book of Luke is the book that is most concerned with the issue of poverty. In his article, *The Lectionary As a Guide to Thinking About Poverty*, Bergen says there have been complete studies conducted on the poverty depicted in Luke's gospel account, and it is a complex question to be answered as Luke uses strange parables about the use of wealth as well as some of the most challenging calls for the complete removal of poverty. Luke's presentation of wealth and poverty is far from simple, and ambiguous at best (Bergen 2014).

The coming of Jesus brought with it a sudden end to the norm and usual way that things were done. Jesus announces, in Luke 4:18-19, the beginning of a new age. That announcement implies that the means and methods of the current system are subpar and are no longer going to be adhered to. Although his message was one of hope and uplift for the poor, there were still those that made it their mission to make sure the poor remained poor; even worse, some wanted to continue to benefit from others' poverty. Jesus spoke to the bonded slaves (referred to as captives), but there were certainly those who had no desire to see the system change.

The ministry of Jesus responded to a threat that was alluded to in his announcement. At the onset of Jesus' announcement of his ministry, his declaration of liberation, jubilee, and the fulfillment of Scripture, was met with outrage by those who were in the synagogue. His ministry involved a complete shift in practice and upheaval of societal norms. In typical fashion, those that profited from the present conditions and practices were the ones that were most resistant to any change that could alter their current state: "Very early Jesus is correctly perceived as a clear and present danger to that order, and this is the problem with the promissory newness of the gospel: it never promises without threatening, it never begins without ending something, it never gives gifts without also assessing harsh costs" (Brueggemann 2001, 84).

Obery Hendricks argues that "Jesus announces that the reason for his anointing by God and the purpose of his mission in the world are one and the same–to proclaim radical economic, social, and political change: "The spirit of the Lord is upon me, because he has anointed me to bring good news to the poor. He has sent me to proclaim release to the captives and recovery of sight to the blind, to let the oppressed go free, to proclaim the year of the Lord's favor" (Luke 4:18-19) (Hendricks 2006, Kindle 175).

The Jesus that Luke describes makes no attempt to hide the radicality of his calling in this passage. He first proclaimed the good news to the poor, using the Greek word for poor, *ptochois*, indicating a collective class or identity (Hendricks 2006, Kindle 175). In other words, he stated that the purpose of his ministry was to bring about a drastic change within the conditions and establishments that kept people oppressed. A radical change was necessary because only a radical change could bring about a real difference in their predicament. His announcement also spoke to the release of the unjustly imprisoned. Considering the sheer number of political prisoners detained in the Roman jails and those who had been forced into poverty because of economic exploitation, this was a proclamation of great magnitude (Hendricks 2006, Kindle 175).

> Then he made the ultimate political pronouncement: he announced liberation to those who were oppressed by the crushing weight of the empire. Not 'bruised,' as some translations render it, but 'oppressed,' from the Greek word *thrawo*, 'oppress, crush.' Jesus ended his inaugural sermon by proclaiming 'the acceptable year of the Lord,' an allusion to the year of Jubilee (Leviticus 25:8-10), the end of a fifty-year cycle, when all land that had been confiscated or otherwise unjustly acquired was to be returned to its original owners. (Hendricks 2006, Kindle 188)

When looked at within the context of Jesus' times, his sermon resembles a manifesto. It is a call to bring about a complete change in economics, politics, and social justice as they relate to his people. It is a call for a comprehensive upheaval to the current system of living. To make a statement more radical than that would be very difficult (Hendricks 2006, Kindle 188).

Hendricks also argues that "Jesus invokes the memory of the Exodus often in the Gospels by repeatedly invoking Moses' name. And just as God declared the oppression of the Hebrews as the motive for divine intervention – his ministry – by choosing the liberation text of Isaiah 61:1-2 as his manifesto: 'The spirit of the Lord…has anointed me…to bring good news to the poor' (Luke 4:18)" (Hendricks 2006, Kindle 292).

Typically, when we read Luke 4:18-19, we don't read it in the same way that the people during Jesus' day would have read it. Those people would more than likely have known about the rest of that passage from which Jesus was quoting. I would like to note that in

Luke, Jesus has a very different public theology than those present in the synagogue on that day. I am always intrigued about what people don't say, and in this particular case, I am intrigued by what Jesus didn't quote. When you read beyond Isaiah 61:1-2 and beyond Luke 4:18-19, you find the essence of what made them so angry to the point they wanted to throw Jesus off a cliff. It is clear that they had a different theology.

CHAPTER 7
RETHINKING OUR THEOLOGY TO HELP THE POOR

It is very important to take note of the fact that the way that a person views the world lays the foundation for the manner in which that person thinks about ethical questions. For many people, the precise manner and timetable in which to help the poor becomes an ethical question. It has often been said that a chain is only as strong as its weakest link. The same could be said of society, as a "community at its best is but a collection of independent individuals" (Copeland 1994, 120). There must be a shift from the old way of thinking and behaving where individuals ultimately strive to advance only their own interests and needs: "The contemporary public issue of poverty requires a contemporary public theology to deal adequately with its complexity" (Copeland 1994, 126). It is rare for there to be a disagreement about the fact that poverty is wrong and needs to be addressed. The tension arises when groups try to come to a consensus on the Scripture or guidelines that should be the basis for policy changes. This is why there is a need for public theology. "This theology needed to state a basic understanding of the meaning and purpose of human life that identified realities like poverty as unjust, without seeking agreement on the more specific theological doctrines that divide people" (Copeland 1994, 126).

We need theological doctrines that will bring us together as a people with a common goal of ending poverty.

Process Theology

It has been my experience that our theology affects our views on poverty. When I was in seminary, I was introduced to the line of thought called Process Theology. This expanded my thought process tremendously. Being able to analyze the issue of poverty through this lens will allow people to expand the way that they view God and God's creation.

God is always greater no matter how great we think God is. Some would argue that most have a half-truth about God. I propose a theology that will allow people to see the whole truth about God. This type of thought shows the grace, mercy, and love of a relational God. Indeed, as scholar and theologian Theodore Walker notes in his book, *Mothership Connections: A Black Atlantic Synthesis of Neoclassical Metaphysics and Black Theology*, "a doctrine of God as God is developed in a variety of constructive postmodern theology indebted to the metaphysics of (Alfred) Whitehead and (Charles) Hartshorn. The variety of postmodern theology is frequently called 'process theology,' and when the emphasis is more Hartshornean than Whiteheadian, it is often called neoclassical theology" (Walker 2004, 25). To help the poor we must have a whole truth about God and a concentrated effort to present a new approach to how we think about those who are oppressed.

It is complicated for the doctrine to be considered sufficient until the obvious assumptions relating to the philosophical and metaethical aspects are brought to light. William R. Jones illustrates this point in his book, *Is God a White Racist?*, and explains the idea that non-liberating visions of God are the results of classical metaphysics (Walker 2004, viii).

Metaphysics can be defined as the "scientific study of logically necessary existential truths" (Walker 2004, 26). Existential truths are the truths that deal with existence and the reality that we live in. When looked at in a broader scope, metaphysics is the scientific study of the truths about existence. Neoclassical metaphysics encompasses the idea of strict metaphysics (Walker 2004, 26).

Charles Hartshorn and those that studied under him developed neoclassical metaphysics. It is a metaphysical philosophy and theology. Charles Hartshorn was under Alfred Whitehead's instruction, and for this reason, neoclassical metaphysics often falls under the umbrella of Whitehead's process philosophy (Walker 2004, 26).

Hartshorne refers to his contributions as "neoclassical." He references both positive and negative reasons for this label. On the positive side, by merging the terms "neo" and "classical," there is an implication of a modification to classical thinking. "Classical Greek and medieval philosophical influences contributed to modern classical theism's theological mistakes, including a mistaken conception of omnipotence" (Walker 2004, 26). Hartshorne's neoclassical thought process is a modified version of that classical theism, called "neoclassical theism." The negative aspect of Hartshorne preferring "neoclassical" over "process" is the way that neoclassical does not put as much emphasis on the actual process, which includes the initial, transition, and change phases. There is however equal attention to relativity, which includes social relations and sharing creativity: "Hartshorne says the term neoclassical is noncommittal with regard to which theme (process or relativity) is more essential to metaphysics" (Walker 2004, 27).

Classical theism is a traditional and widely accepted form of theology. There is a great need to reframe the manner in which God is viewed. The reason we need to reframe the ways in which God is viewed is because it causes division. For example, throughout American history Jesus has been painted as a white, blue-eyed male. We know this is not true, but places like Hollywood and even some churches continue to paint this picture. Because of this narrative of Jesus, it is easy for some to see God as white. If you think Jesus is white, that means that in your theology you could see God as being white; this would make some believe that whiteness is dominant, and this causes a divide based on theology. Theology can be dangerous as we have seen with the evangelical church in recent years. I believe this example proves that we don't know the whole truth about God. In the process of reframing these views, it is possible to move towards a more neoclassical standpoint where one is able to get a more complete view of who God is. The thought that God is "perfect," as in the classical view, leads to the belief that God cannot and will not change, because the need for or occurrence of change implies the presence of faults. This represents an incomplete view of God. "Where in the Bible God is spoken of as perfect, the indications are then even here the exclusion of change in every respect was not implied" (Hartshorne 2007, 2). A neoclassical theological view sees that God has the ability to change when it is necessary, and this change does not alter that perfection. Even the term "neoclassical" implies a revision and not a replacement of classical thinking (Walker 2004, 26). Neoclassical theology is a revised idea of God. In this thought process, God is emphasized as "God as God of all creation," including the oppressed (Walker 2004, 25).

By emphasizing necessary divine absolutes and denying or ignoring divine relativity, the single transcendence of classical theism produces a supremely anti-social (nonrelative) conception of God – God as a wholly other, immutable, unmoved mover. On the other hand, the dual transcendence of neoclassical theism yields a supremely social-relational conception of God because it enables us to conceive God as a supreme person (33).

Before moving further, it is important to show examples that Charles Hartshorn gives of the differences between classical and neoclassical:

- "Classical theism affirms divine immutability and denies divine change; neoclassical theism on the other hand affirms both, with change including immutable aspects."
- "Classical theism's conception of divine omnipotence errs in holding that God is wholly determinative of all actual events. Neoclassical theism omnipotence means God is partly determinative of all actual events, and partly determinative by all actual events; where, by contrast, less powerful entities are partly determinative of some actual events, and partly determined by some actual events."
- "Classical theism's conception of divine omniscience wrongly holds that whatever happens must have been eternally known as wholly predetermined in every respect by God. Neoclassical theology holds that omniscience means all-knowing and knowing all things as they really are means knowing the actually determined as actually determined and knowing the fully not yet determined (not yet actual) as not yet fully determined."
- "The classical conception of divine goodness wrongly holds that God is impassible or unsympathetic, an 'unmoved mover' who does not suffer. Neoclassical theology holds that divine goodness includes supreme and unsurpassable sympathy. The all-inclusive one experiences every experience, suffering every pain and joyfully."

- "Classical theism frequently errs in conceiving of human immortality as 'a career after death.' Instead of the classical view of 'subjective immortality' as a never ending, after death career, Hartshorne holds to a Whiteheadian doctrine of 'objective immortality' according to which 'an entire career, with all its concrete values, is an imperishable possession of deity.'"
- "Classical theism is marked by the erroneous conception of infallible special revelation. Logically, divinely inspired humans cannot produce wholly infallible documents or doctrines because any synthesis of the wholly infallible and the partly fallible must yield a partly fallible product" (Walker 2004, 34).

According to the book *Essentials of Christian Theology*, process theologians argue that traditional theologians have "lost sight of the God of compassion we encounter in the Bible and put too much emphasis on a God of power and control. They define God, in Whitehead's phrases, as 'the poet of the world, with tender patience leading it by his vision of truth, beauty, and goodness'." (Grenz and Placher 2003, 55). It goes on to define God as the "great companion," one who suffers alongside us, and also understands. According to process theology, the characteristics of God as changing, evolving, and being involved in human suffering contribute to God's perfection rather than threaten it like the view of Aristotle (Grenz and Placher 2003, 56).

Grace, Mercy and Love Liberate Us

Donald Mckim (1996) defines grace, mercy, and love in this way:

- Grace - "God's grace is extended to sinful humanity in providing salvation and forgiveness through Jesus Christ that is not deserved and withholding the judgment that is deserved. The unmerited favor of God." (Mckim 1996, 120)

- Mercy - "Kind and compassionate treatment extending biblically to forgiveness and the gracious bestowal of that which is not deserved." (Mckim 1996, 171)
- Love - "A strong feeling of personal affection, care, desire for the well-being of others." (Mckim 1996, 164)

In *A Black Theology of Liberation*, James Cone (2010) says, "The Christian understanding of God arises from the biblical view of revelation, a revelation of God takes place in the liberation of oppressed Israel and is completed in the incarnation, in Jesus Christ. This means whatever is said about the nature of God and God being in the world must be based on the biblical account of God's revelatory activity" (64). He also adds, "The black theology of God must be of the God who is participating in the liberation of the oppressed of the land. Because God has been revealed in the history of oppressed Israel and decisively in the oppressed One, Jesus Christ, it is impossible to say anything about God without seeing God as being involved in the contemporary liberation of all oppressed peoples" (Cone 2010, 64).

Therefore, we should have compassion and not exclude any of our brothers and sisters. In his book, *God and the Excluded*, Joerg Rieger gives us examples and models from several theologians. The models of Self, Wholly Other, Language and Text, and Turn to Others are all good models, but each can be problematic. However, I like the idea of using the strengths of all four models to construct a balanced theological approach (Rieger 2001). The great thing about God is that God gives us all the ability to see the truth. If God is personal, relational, and merciful, we as God's creations should seek to put ourselves in the shoes of others, because it's only then that we will understand that we must not exclude, but we must liberate others.

Liberating Love

Cone states that Jesus Christ is "God himself coming into the very depths of human existence for the sole purpose of striking off the chains of slavery, thereby freeing man from ungodly principles and powers that hinder his relationship with God" (Cone 1997, 35). Luke 4:18-19 reads: "The Spirit of the Lord is upon me, because he has anointed me to bring good news to the poor. He has sent me to proclaim release to the captives and recovery of sight to the blind, to let the oppressed go free, to proclaim the year of the Lord's favor" (NRSV).

Jesus came to bring liberation. Becoming a slave, he understands the full capacity of what it is like to be human. Therefore, the gospel itself is a gospel of liberation for those who are oppressed. Jesus' work did not stop two thousand years ago, but even now in the twenty-first century, Jesus is still proclaiming release to the captives, recovery of sight to the blind, and letting the oppressed go free. Jesus continues the fight against injustice. Cone states it this way: "If he is not in the ghetto, if he is not where men are living at the brink of existence, but is, rather in the easy life of the suburbs, then the gospel is a lie" (Cone 1997, 38).

Jesus came to bring freedom. Galatians 5:1 tells us, "For freedom Christ has set us free. Stand firm, therefore, and do not submit again to a yoke of slavery." It is freedom that allows us to serve God totally and freely. The good news of freedom is that God has set us free, and we are no longer slaves. As John 8:36 proclaims, "So, if the Son makes you free, you will be free indeed." This means since Jesus has set us free from oppression, we have an obligation to set others free and to follow the examples of Jesus. We must create solutions to stop poverty.

The Creator's Response to Creation

It is important to understand that God the Creator continues to create presently in our everyday lives—constantly creating situations that influence creation's decision-making. We are a part of creation, and we cannot escape the created order because we are creatures and it is here, both on earth and in heaven, that we live and serve God. Situations are always changing, and we experience this in our every-day reality. We experience the reality that past events contribute to present events and that present events contribute to future events. Therefore, we make a creative contribution to the creative synthetic process which means the past is never determinative of what happens next (Walker 2014).

God Liberates Through Grace, Mercy, and Love

God the "Creator," through grace, mercy, and love, liberated Adam and Eve in the Garden of Eden. Humanity did not die; instead, God made provisions for Adam and Eve to live outside of the garden but not out of fellowship. Since the beginning, God as the "Creator" has always taken a little bit of this and a little bit of that and created something new (Walker 2014). Therefore, God is the "Creator" who is constantly creating. God liberated humanity through Jesus Christ and God continued that liberation through the working of the Holy Spirit.

Creation was not a one-time event. It is always in process. God creates the creature and creatures create. Creativity is a process and is always going on. According to John 5:16-17, "Therefore, the Jews started persecuting Jesus, because he was doing such things on the Sabbath. But Jesus answered them, 'My Father is still working, and I also am working.'" Because of our free will, this ongoing process of events is always changing how we experience God's liberating power.

Practicing Grace, Mercy, and Love

Jesus gave us two important commandments in Matthew 22:34-40: Love the Lord your God with all your heart, your soul, and your mind and love your neighbor as yourself. Love my neighbor as myself is a realistic statement. You don't need theology to do justice, but you need theology to do love. As humanity, we have a responsibility to respond to all of God's creation with grace, mercy, and love.

Called to be Set Apart through Grace, Mercy, and Love

The Christian Church is called to be separate from the world. The Holy Spirit empowers the church to live a holy life through surrender to Christ, sanctified in Jesus Christ, and made holy. As such, we live in the world, but should not conduct ourselves like the world. We should be holy, set apart for God's use.

Rodney Clapp argues in *A Peculiar People: The Church as Culture in a Post-Christian Society* that the church needs to reclaim its place in this society as peculiar people. He believes the church in the twenty-first century has merged into the state, and although people would like to think of the church as the center of society, western thinking no longer views the church as being the center of importance (Clapp 1996, 12-19). In *Divided by Faith: Evangelical Religion and the Problem of Race in America,* Emerson and Smith on the other hand believe we have become a "racialized society" (2001, 7) in terms that "evangelicals desire to end racial division and equality and attempt to think and act accordingly but in the process do more to perpetuate the racial divide than they do to tear it down" (Emerson and Smith 2001, Preface).

Arguably the problem of the church is that the church has been defined using basic metaphors such as the body of Christ, the people of God, and the temple of the Holy Spirit. Throughout Christianity, people have tried to use these metaphors to measure the church. I believe that this is mainly due to the interpretation or misinterpretation of Scripture. Therefore, the church has yet to become what it was intended to become. Over time, the church became an institution, and we as people have become institutionalized. Rather than defining ourselves as the church, we define the institution as the church. As a result, the church has been unable to agree on a universal definition.

This explains why we are losing our identity and mission. If you cannot define who you are, it becomes hard to define where you are going. It is our history and society that disrupts our relationship with God because we have no unity and therefore cannot do what we've been called to do for the Kingdom of God. We must rethink our theology to help the poor so we can fix what has been broken.

CHAPTER 8

THE HOUSING CRISIS

The United States housing crisis did not magically appear in 2020 with the coronavirus pandemic. Prior to the pandemic, there were reports of unstable housing in up to 15 percent of households. Record numbers of unemployment only compounded the problems, with one in three Americans reportedly not paying rent in April of 2020, while some continued to be evicted despite the legislation outlined in the CARES Act (Despard 2020).

In April 2020, the Social Policy Institute at Washington University in St. Louis conducted a survey, with findings showing that during the pandemic there was an increase in evictions, delayed rent and mortgage payments, and unexpected utility payments and home repairs. Figure 1 shows that the Hispanic/Latinx populations were more likely than white populations to be evicted, be low-income, and become infected with COVID-19. (Despard 2020)

Figure 1. Eviction experienced during the COVID-19 Pandemic

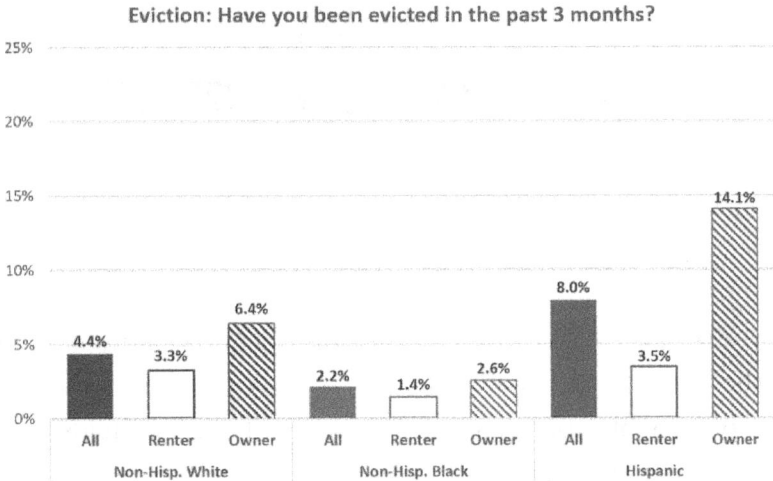

Source: *COVID-19 Survey, Wave 1 (Apr 22, 2020 – May 12, 2020), Social Policy Institute.*
Notes: LMI only. N=2,680.

Figures 1, 2 and 3 summarize the difficulties faced by low-middle
-income homeowners during a three-month period:
- "Twenty percent of Hispanic/Latinx homeowners did not pay
  the full amount of their mortgage, which is nearly two times
  greater than the entire sample (10.4 percent) during the COVID
  19 Pandemic (Figure 2)."
- "One in five LMI (low and moderate income) Hispanic/Latinx
  homeowners skipped a bill or paid a bill late (Figure 2)."
- "Seventeen percent of these individuals had an unexpected
  major house or appliance repair, straining their already tenuous
  financial situation during the pandemic (Figure 3)."

In addition to homeowners, renters have been especially hit hard
by the pandemic. Historically, LMI renters face great challenges
in finding affordable housing, sometimes spending over half their

income on housing alone. COVID-19 has exacerbated this crisis (Despard 2020).

Figure 2. Delinquency experienced during the COVID-19 Pandemic

Delinquency: Have you been behind on rent/mortgage
in the past 3 months?

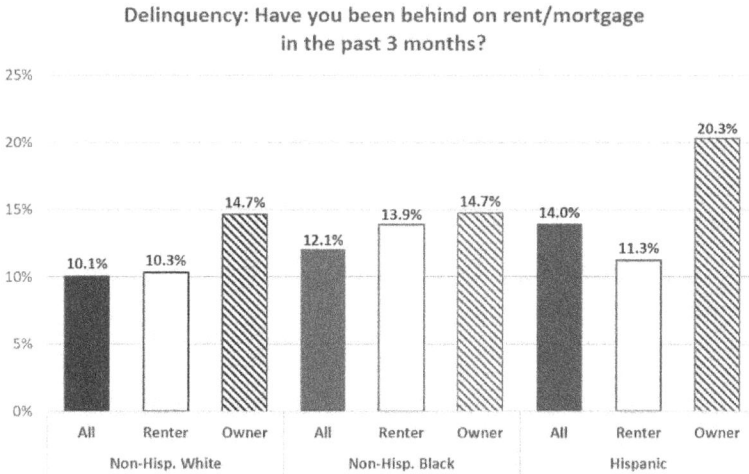

Source: COVID-19 Survey, Wave 1 (Apr 22, 2020 – May 12, 2020), Social Policy Institute.
Notes: LMI only. N=2,672.

Figure 3. Utility payment delay and major home repairs during the COVID-19 Pandemic

Utility Payment Delay & Major Home Repairs

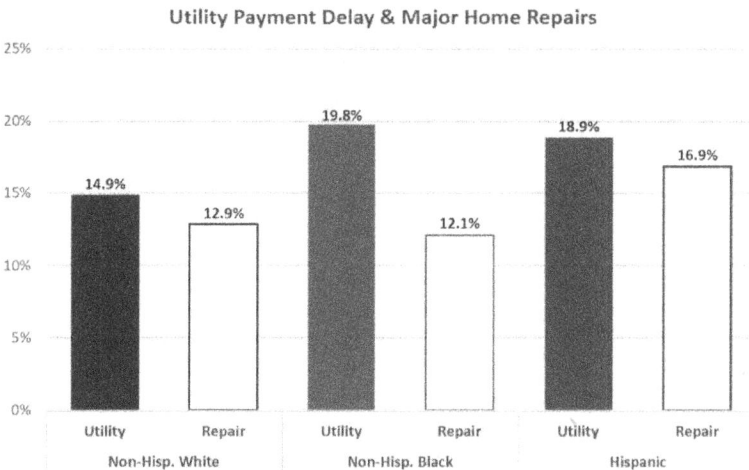

Source: COVID-19 Survey, Wave 1 (Apr 22, 2020 – May 12, 2020), Social Policy Institute.
Notes: LMI only. N=2,677.

People who depend on rental properties for their living quarters are less likely to have funds set aside to be used in the case of an emergency or unplanned event like a pandemic. More than 40 percent of the low- and moderate-income households surveyed did not have any emergency funds set aside. Unfortunately, there is a high probability that even more people will be affected when they are no longer receiving unemployment benefits (Despard 2020).

Moving from a "Band-aid" to a Long-Term Solution

On March 27, 2020, the United States Senate signed into law a coronavirus aid package that was intended to provide financial relief to those low-income individuals that had been affected most. This law, known as the CARES Act (Coronavirus Aid Relief and Economic Security), provided a temporary fix to a problem that had been persistent long before the coronavirus pandemic and would continue to hinder people after the pandemic. The low- and middle-income families in need of the relief promised by the act experienced long wait times in receiving their aid (Despard 2020).

Despite the fact that the CARES Act included legislation to prevent evictions on a federal level, that relief was not as widespread as needed and will likely run out long before individuals have fully recovered from the pandemic (Despard 2020).

Figure 4. Receipt of CARES Act benefits during the COVID-19 Pandemic

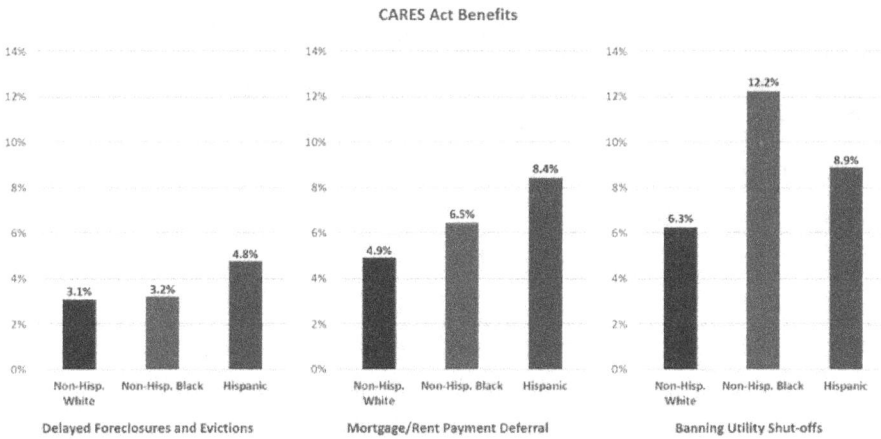

CARES Act Benefits

Source: COVID-19 Survey, Wave 1 (Apr 22, 2020 – May 12, 2020), Social Policy Institute.
Notes: LMI only. N=2,680.

While the CARES Act was supposed to provide relief for those individuals who needed it most, there were certain limitations, hindering widespread aid, instead narrowing relief to specific types of housing. Limitations also prevented it from extending relief to all renters and homeowners for the length of time that the aid was actually needed (Despard 2020).

Existing Housing Crisis

Low-income populations are well accustomed to housing hardships. Housing that is in poor condition, trying to accommodate multiple generations under one roof, coupled with limited access to healthy food and healthcare services, are problems that have been further intensified by the coronavirus pandemic. These housing conditions lead to a greater risk of COVID-19 infection as well as underlying ailments that greatly increase the risks of negative effects of the virus (Despard 2020).

The findings of the April 2020 survey by the Social Policy Institute at Washington University in St. Louis make a case that certain groups are disproportionately impacted, facing higher rates of housing hardship than other groups. The Latinx/Hispanic populations are severely affected. Other affected populations include persons recently released from prison and those most likely to expedite the spread of the virus simply because they are living in crowded households and are more likely to have been exposed to the virus (Despard 2020).

Adequate and quality housing is something that all people deserve, regardless of their income level. The coronavirus pandemic has magnified the inequalities that already existed among low- and moderate-income populations. There is a great need for legislators to authorize policies that provide access to quality housing, especially in this time when communities are struggling to recover from this pandemic (Despard 2020).

The recession caused by the COVID-19 Pandemic is unparalleled with any event in modern U.S. history. It has highlighted the reality that low-income, particularly low-income *minority* populations, are more likely to experience job loss and be exposed to health risks (Qureshi 2020).

Unbalanced Income

While we have seen an increase in income inequality in the majority of advanced economies in the world in recent decades, the increase has been particularly glaring in the United States. Middle-class wage earners are feeling the pressure, and the average worker has been experiencing prolonged cycles of stationary wage scales (Qureshi 2020).

The social, political, and economic ramifications of this upshift in inequality are unfavorable, to say the least. The fires of social discontent, political polarization, and populist nationalism are being fueled at alarming rates (Qureshi 2020).

CHAPTER 9

EMPOWERMENT

If we have any hope of managing disasters such as the COVID-19 Pandemic, we must have a clear vision of a community where neighbors are well acquainted and engage in open dialogue about their visions for the future (Fullilove 2016, 237 Kindle).

By highlighting deficiencies in various communities, the pandemic has presented us with the opportunity to develop communities that will provide all the necessary resources to aid all people within it and help those who may be in poverty.

Below I will attempt to show two examples that prove that it is possible to renew a sense of Beloved Community by changing the narrative of poverty and gentrification. This can be done by rebuilding and building the village through empowering people, the poor and the marginalized. These are just two of many examples of how we can create long-lasting, sustainable, Beloved Communities.

Dudley Street Neighborhood Initiative

Dudley Street is an example of how an impoverished community in Roxbury, Massachusetts collectively took back its neighborhood and changed its own condition. According to the Dudley Street Neighborhood Initiative, their mission is "to empower Dudley residents to organize, plan for, create and control a vibrant, diverse and high-quality neighborhood in collaboration with community partners" (DSNI n.d.).

The Dudley Street Neighborhood Initiative (DSNI) has been around for more than 35 years; it began in 1984. Their first organizing campaign came in 1986, and the Dudley Neighbors Community Land Trust (CLT) was created in 1988. They broke ground for the first new CLT housing in 1993. That same year, they launched their three strategic focus areas with the goal of maximizing impact as an economic power, resident leadership, and youth opportunities and development. In 2012, they were one of seven neighborhoods in the country to receive a US Department of Education Promise Neighborhoods implementation grant. They released their new strategic vision in 2018 (DSNI n.d.).

DSNI was established by residents of Dudley, with the goal of reclaiming the neighborhood that had been nearly destroyed by arson, dumping, and lack of investments. Neighbors and residents took it upon themselves to devise an all-inclusive plan to restore their community. By gaining eminent domain authority, DSNI was able to secure development, purchase vacant land, and protect the affordability of the area: "The road that DSNI traveled in obtaining eminent domain authority was essentially a community organizing process that built its strength from the bottom up" ("Dudley Street Neighborhood Initiative"). Canvassing neighborhoods, knocking on doors, garnering support from residents and business leaders, allowed for the establishment of a stronger presence in city politics.

At the forefront of the development of the community was the arduous task of addressing problems that impacted day-to-day living, like the illegal dumping that stained the cityscape. By addressing issues like this first, DSNI was able to gain community support, while at the same time building a foundation of leadership within the neighborhood. Success in these endeavors resulted in the residents having greater confidence in their own political skills and a realization of the extent of the power that they could harness simply by working and speaking collectively ("Dudley Street Neighborhood Initiative").

The visible improvements as well as the increased civic involvement of the Dudley residents have extended benefits into various facets of the community, life there, and its residents: "DSNI's democratic model of community planning and development produces stability in the community" (Dudley Street Neighborhood Initiative). Low-income renters in this Boston-area neighborhood do not live in fear of gentrification caused by wealthier land and business owners moving in and taking over their community. Businesses that desire to establish themselves in the community undergo a vetting process to ensure that they aim to serve the best interests and address the needs of the residents. Businesses and services organizations are held to a high standard of community involvement and engagement, ensuring that everyone is held accountable for contributing to the long-term success of the community (Dudley Street Neighborhood Initiative).

The DSNI Board is composed of residents that led the community through a democratically elected community process. This system has led to increased civic participation, economic opportunities, connections within the community, and numerous opportunities for the youth of the community. By investing in the youth of the community, the youth have become encouraged to reciprocate by investing in the community. The diversities of race, ethnicities, language, and race have been embraced and become the foundation of the community (DSNI n.d.). In order to make its mission a reality, DSNI has four key focus areas that drive its work within the community.

Development without Displacement works to ensure that current residents are not displaced by new incoming businesses and strives to promote the culture of the neighborhood. This is achieved by utilizing community land use planning, preserving and supporting the creation of affordable housing, taking leadership at the city level to drive policy change, and expanding the Community Land Trust model through partnership and collaboration with various city and regional organizations in the surrounding Greater Boston community (DSNI n.d.).

The main premise of **Youth Voice** is to nurture the next generation of leaders, preparing them to lead in the community and beyond. The youth have the opportunity to design and lead campaigns reflective of the interests and needs of the youth. They are provided with opportunities and training to foster leadership qualities and experiences (DSNI n.d.).

Neighborhood Development is crucial, as DSNI is the leader for community development enterprises in Dudley that encourage collaboration among residents as they strive to rejuvenate the community. Through this focus area, residents are advocates for greater access to public resources, provided opportunities to build assets and wealth, organized, and empowered to collaboratively improve schools in the neighborhood. Residents are equipped to use vacant land and repurpose it to be used as a way to provide access to locally grown, healthy food (DSNI n.d.).

Finally, **Resident Empowerment** aims at strengthening resident capacity. This includes assisting them in becoming engaged in elections and other civic activities and providing training and meaningful leadership opportunities where the board is composed of members of the community who have been adequately prepared for their roles (DSNI n.d.).

All of this has paved the way for family stability as well as the conception of a community land trust. Where there was once destitution, there now exists affordable housing, parks, playgrounds, community facilities, and thriving businesses. As Jay Walljasper notes in his review of *When Activists Win: The Renaissance of Dudley St. The Nation,* "The overriding theme of Dudley Street applies anywhere: The people living in a neighborhood were called on to make the decisions about its future. And they responded with enthusiasm, outrage, hope, creativity, patience and lots of energy" (Walljasper 1997).

The second model is a faith-based one to show faith-based organizations, and specifically, the church, a way they can help change the narrative of gentrification and poverty in their own communities.

Mission Waco

According to Mission Waco, their mission is to "Provide Christian-based, holistic, relationship-based programs that empower the poor and marginalized. Mobilize middle-class Americans to become more compassionately involved among the poor. Seek ways to overcome the systemic issues of social injustice which oppress the poor and marginalized." In 1978, Jimmy and Janet Dorrell moved into a run-down home in the middle of a declining neighborhood in north Waco, Texas. They felt a calling to live among the poor and use relationships and empowerment opportunities to spread the "good news." They began by opening their home to host weekly clubs for teens and children, meeting their neighbors, and beginning the relationship building. Shortly after that move, they had the opportunity to travel around the world, through which they became increasingly more aware of the needs of the poor, hungry, and unevangelized. They felt pulled back to Waco, Texas where they felt they could serve the Christian students at Baylor University and local churches, as well as the growing number of residents struggling with poverty. In 1991, after years of an informal neighborhood ministry, Mission Waco was founded by a Christian foundation (Christian Mission Concerns), with the Dorrells as the leaders (Mission Waco, Mission World ~ Waco, TX n.d.).

73

There are three main goals that serve as the foundation for Mission Waco Mission World: teaching empowerment through relationship-based, holistic programs among the poor and marginalized, mobilizing middle-class Christians toward "hands-on" involvement, and addressing systemic issues which dis-empower the poor. What began as several programs targeting children and teens, quickly grew to address other needs of the community as the organization accrued more volunteers, interns, and donations. The organization is overseen by a board consisting of twenty Christian men and women from different churches (Mission Waco, Mission World ~ Waco, TX n.d.).

In the early 1990s, Mission Waco was able to purchase several buildings surrounding the Dorrells' home. As funds and volunteers allowed, Mission Waco continued to acquire and renovate several businesses which had been attracting negative activity. When these renovations were complete, they introduced the Jubilee Center to the community. This establishment provided job training, computer labs, GED classes, community empowerment programs, and a theater housing 200 seats for dance, drama, community meetings, and a large climbing wall. The old bar next to the Jubilee Center is now known as Alpha Quest and is used for various children and youth programs. Since its early days, Mission Waco has grown and expanded to provide many additional services to the surrounding community. They include but are not limited to:

- Church Under the Bridge – meets under the Interstate 35 underpass near Baylor University, serving approximately 300 people per week
- Manna House – residential alcohol/drug recovery home
- The Lighthouse – transition house for those completing the program at Manna House

- My Brother's Keeper – shelter for emergency housing for chronically homeless adult men and women
- The Ark Apartments – mixed-income Christians living in a program-based living center with spiritual mentoring and accountability
- Mission Waco Health Clinic – serving the poor with acute care by volunteer doctors, dentists, nurses, chiropractors, orthopedic doctors, etc.
- Jubilee Food Market – a non-profit local food market designed to address the reality of our neighborhood being a "food desert" with a lack of fresh foods and affordable groceries for purchase
- The Clothesline – a stylish boutique selling women's clothing
- Urban Reap (Renewable Energy and Agricultural Project) – Farm to Table, Aquaponics, Compost, Rain Harvesting, Tools, Supplies, Resources (Mission Waco, Mission World ~ Waco, TX n.d.).

Since the very beginning, Mission Waco (which became Mission Waco Mission World in 2012) has invited members of the community to foster relationships with the poor and local churches. The Dorrells' vision of spreading "the good news" to the poor continues to live on through the services provided and they continue to be faithful to their original desire of using a biblical base for empowering compassion.

CHAPTER 10
BUILDING A COMMUNITY

Sustainability

According to Warren Flint in his book, *Practice of Sustainable Community Development: A Participatory Framework for Change,* the process of creating a community that is sustainable must take into account the countless hours of scientific study that have yielded results regarding the connections and influences between social behaviors and all the factors that influence the survival, development, and evolution of the community (Flint 2013, 4). Planning for a future that is sustainable requires that a community is willing to compromise regarding the specific needs that need to be addressed in the present, how addressing those needs will affect the future people and conditions, and what type of accommodations they are willing to make in order to plan for the best possible outcomes.

This may require making some adjustments to lifestyles of the community, and these adjustments have to be accepted by the present members of the community as well as align with their values, while also not jeopardizing the opportunities of the future generations. In more basic terms, sustainability requires the community to distinguish between essential desires, and come to a common understanding of what is enough. This collective and mutual understanding allows for a clearer vision of adjusting the present to provide for a better future (Flint 2013, 4).

A Sense of Community

A community is built where there is an assembling of people who grow to trust and depend on both each other and the land which they inhabit. As the people change, the landscape changes and vice versa. These changes are in part due to the evolving relationships present in the community. The shared identity of the community, which is "grounded in its history, which must be passed from one generation to the next if the community is to know itself throughout the passage of time" (Flint 2013, 5). When there is a disruption in the relationship that the people have with the land, the damage is done to the connection between the two and this can cause the way that the people view the land to be altered. Where there was once a mutually beneficial association, there may now exist a separation, and people "may begin to view its landscape as a separate commodity to be exploited for immediate financial gain" (Flint 2013, 5). This separation causes a great divide in the community resulting in inward destruction. It is ultimately the responsibility of the community to determine what ideals are non-negotiable and the manner in which they will be protected.

In order to live sustainably, the community must identify their essential necessities, both material and not, and develop a plan for how to retain them without imposing needless restrictions on the community both present and future. Only then can they maintain what is essential for living through time, as well as guarantee that future generations will be able to reap the benefits established by the community (Flint 2013, 5).

Communities are places where people live and work both individually and collectively, comprising the actual community. If they are not places where people desire to live and have the ability to thrive, then being sustainable is impossible, no matter how 'green' those places may be. The connection between community and sustainability comes from the basis that without quality relationships and a strong sense of community, there would be little to no chance of a collaborative effort to bring about the "pro-environmental behavioral change" that is necessary (Meltzer 2005, 1).

According to Meltzer, "The concept of sustainability originated in the early 1970s, being first articulated in the influential paper, "Blueprint for Survival," published in the journal, *The Ecologist*. The introduction to "Blueprint" commenced with these words: 'The principle defect of the industrial way of life is that it is not sustainable'" (Meltzer 2005, 1). The authors go on to describe that it is unsustainable due to the rapid population growth and accompanying superfluous consumption of materials. In this work, the authors use the terms "sustainable" and "stable" interchangeably (Meltzer 2005, 1).

In the years since the term sustainable was first introduced, it has been used by many, and like most terms it has been used in various ways, often being manipulated in order to serve the interests of those using it. It has been used by biologists and economists in reference to the impact of humans on ecosystems and natural environments respectively (Meltzer 2005, 1).

The more frequently that the term is used to serve different purposes, the more diluted its meaning becomes. For the purpose of this discussion, we will use Meltzer's basic definition: "able to be maintained at a certain level" (Meltzer 2005, 1). This definition aligns with the widely accepted definition proposed by the United Nations World Commission on Environment and Development, that is, "meeting the needs of the present, without compromising the ability of future generations to meet their own needs" (Meltzer 2005, 1).

There are also many variations in the definitions of community. "The classical definition incorporates three essential characteristics:

social interaction, shared ties and common geographical location, but implies other attributes such as human-scale, belonging, obligation, gemeinschaft etc.," (Meltzer 2005, 2). Gemeinschaft is a word akin to community and social relationships. If we focus on the first two elements of this definition, community can be regarded as:

> a certain quality or measure of social interaction within a group and the shared ties or common interests of its members. Words, such as 'common', 'community', 'commune', 'communitarianism', 'communalism' and 'communism' originate from the French, *communer*, meaning 'to share.' The French word in fact derives from the Latin, communis; com meaning 'with' and *munius* meaning 'duties.' Thus, sharing is fundamental to community, as are close relationships and the notion of commitment (Meltzer 2005, 2).

In order to achieve sustainable Beloved Community, the community must draw upon its common interests, needs, resources and abilities, and develop a plan to maximize them in a way that will withstand time.

Greed versus Sustainability

There were many factors in addition to urban renewal that contributed to the breaking down of communities. African Americans were among many groups of citizens that were affected. Cities are continually restructured by the construction of new highways, gentrification, and economic restructuring. By nature, cities will change, grow, and transform with the passage of time. There are multiple factors that contribute to these transformations, and unfortunately, they do not all yield positive results. Complete and unrestrained greed is a factor that is most likely to lead to catastrophe. Sustainability is most likely to yield the most positive results. It stands to reason, then, that people who are greedy are strictly opposed to sustainability because while sustainability results in long-term success and survival, it takes away from the immediate gratification that greedy people seek (Fullilove 2016, 236 Kindle).

Community Economic Development

According to *The Community Economic Development Handbook: Strategies and Tools to Revitalize Your Neighborhood*, author Mihailo Temali writes that most groups attempting to build community economic development focus on the same major tenets: creating economic opportunity, reversing negative perceptions, and stimulating purchases and investments. This is occurring in African American communities, Native American communities, and communities of recent immigrants. Regardless of the composition of the communities, the goal is to make economic progress in the neighborhood by improving the economic status of the residents and bringing about noticeable changes that result in a community that is a better place to live (Temali 2012, 163 Kindle).

Community economic development is the total package of bringing together all facets of the community. This development encompasses the people, land, money, businesses, talents, and living conditions of all members of the community. It is more than "fixing" the buildings and businesses, and it is certainly not about replacing the lower-income residents with residents who have higher incomes in order to stimulate the economy. Community economic development takes into account what is currently available in the community and strategizes ways to maximize the strengths. This is done with the ultimate goal of bringing about changes that result in a community that is economically strong and has community members that realize the collective value of their neighbors (Temali 2012, 163 Kindle).

Consider this definition of community economic development:

> Actions taken by an organization representing an urban neighborhood or rural community in order to 1. Improve the economic situation of local residents (disposable income and assets and local businesses (profitability and growth); and 2. Enhance the community's quality of life as a whole (appearance, safety, networks, gathering places, and sense of positive momentum). This definition captures the two key goals of community economic development. (Temali 2012, 172 Kindle)

When one is looking at the concept of economic well-being, it is natural for members of a community to focus on the status of their own individual family. This usually includes being able to afford basic material goods, being able to regularly pay bills, and hopefully having something left to live off of after the bills are paid. Let's not forget the ability to save something for those inevitable emergencies that will arise (Temali 2012, 172 Kindle). However, all of this is "survival" in its most basic sense and does not account for a complete picture of community development. All of these factors fail to take into account the condition of the community as a whole, which is just as important. On the other side of evaluating the strength of the community, it is important to take into account the perceptions and thoughts about the community that the people of the community hold. Their feelings about the community's potential to flourish in the future, the extent to which they feel connected as community members, and their perceptions about the visual appeal of the neighborhood, are just as important as their economic daily lives. Community economic development aims to improve the conditions for the individuals and the community as a whole (Temali 2012, 181 Kindle).

When there is an increase in the economic standard for low-income residents in low-income neighborhoods, individuals and families are impacted and have some sort of income remaining after they have paid for their necessities (Temali 2012, 181 Kindle). The community is impacted when the community as a whole becomes more livable. By establishing new places for the community to socialize as well as spend their money, the economic foundation is strengthened, and this contributes to the social health of the community. Community pride is enhanced when there are improvements made that increase the visual appeal of the community. When local business ownership is promoted, there is a greater chance that local members of the community will be able to remain in the community, serving as role models, as well as providing employment for members of the community (Temali 2012, 192 Kindle).

It is important to note the differences between community economic development that actually involves the community in the development process and those processes that are undertaken solely by the private or public sector. Community economic development aims to impact both the individual and the community as a whole. When individuals are more self-sufficient and economically stable, they are more able to contribute positively to the community, thus the community benefits by being collectively stronger. In this model, the community members are invested in the continuing development and success of that one particular community. They are in control of the planning and implementation and the ultimate outcomes of their collective efforts (Temali 2012, 192 Kindle). Eugene "Gus" Newport, a social justice activist, former MLK fellow at Massachusetts Institute of Technology (MIT), and member of the National Council of Elders – an organization that engages leaders of the twentieth-century civil rights movement to share what they have learned with this generation's young leaders, says "look at the community economic development holistically. Don't just develop any type of business without taking into consideration the makeup of the neighborhood, the job skills of residents, and your overall community development goals" (Temali 2012, 202 Kindle).

Empowerment

Empowerment is a concept that surfaces most frequently amidst discussions around any processes of social change. It deals with the confrontation between those who hold prevailing power and those who are considered common people in societies. While there are many definitions, they all seem to fall in line with this definition put forth by the Cornell Empowerment group: "[Empowerment is] an intentional ongoing process centered in local community, involving mutual respect, critical reflection, caring and group participation, through which people lacking an equal share of valued resources gain greater access to and control over those resources" (Meltzer 2005, 2). When the individuals of a community come together with a sense of collaboration, they are able to participate in comprehensive control over their circumstances and lives in general, empowering each other within their own community. This is closely entwined with the idea of community development where this collaboration results in communal efficiency (Meltzer 2005, 2).

Three Faces of Empowerment

In recent years, when discussing community development, the term empowerment has become a bit of a catchphrase. It has been an attention-grabbing term strategically inserted in brochures and discussions regarding community leadership and on the minds of community developers. It is for this very reason that it is important to explore the meaning and interpretation of empowerment, as well as look at different types and the ways that its connotation can enhance the success of community development. Empowerment generally means to give power to another, to provide the means of exerting or asserting power as a behavior practiced by individuals (Brennan 2015, 33).

According to sociologist and professor emeritus Kenneth E. Pigg, when looking at the idea of empowerment, there are typically three distinct "faces" that are examined: the first face, self-empowerment through individual action, relies on individuals gaining self-efficacy or personal power by gaining a sense of control over their own destiny (Brennan 2015, 35). In this version of empowerment, there is more emphasis on the individual and motivation of the individual as op-posed to a version that relies on the distribution of power. Individuals "who help themselves are generally considered to be empowered" (Brennan 2015, 36). When organizations attempt to empower employees, it is imperative that they address both feelings (belief systems), and skills (management, communication, and influencing) of the employees. By providing opportunities for employees to develop their skills and feelings in relation to the organization, they provide opportunities for them to become empowered.

The second aspect of empowerment is empowerment in organizations and is rooted in the group rather than the individual. A primary responsibility of those in positions of power is to empower or strengthen others. When individuals have the ability to control their own work, collaborate with others in order to effectively complete a task, and respond to external stimuli in a manner that results in maximum productivity, the organization is able to capitalize on its fullest potential and both the individuals and the organization realize empowerment (Brennan 2015, 36).

The third and final aspect of empowerment is found in social institutions and social action. This aspect of empowerment is missing the personal dimension present in the previous two aspects of empowerment. In this aspect of empowerment, disadvantaged populations are given greater control over their own destinies when barriers in political, social, and economic systems are removed (Brennan 2015, 37). Empowerment comes from a collective building of strength, where people who are dependent are connected with people who have the resources that are needed in order to influence change. In its most simple sense, "empowerment is viewed in this context as social action designed to gain access to the power held by others usually in the form of control of resources" (Brennan 2015, 38). When communities are willing to fight on their own behalf or accept the support of those willing to advocate on their behalf, it is possible to become empowered and bring about change.

CHAPTER 11

MARTIN LUTHER KING, JR. ON ABOLISHING POVERTY

Rev. Dr. Martin Luther King, Jr. brought forth the concept that he calls the "Beloved Community" early in his ministry and community-organizing. The term was originally coined by philosopher and theologian Josiah Royce and was popularized by King. This idea of community steps away from the current "neoliberal conceptions of community" and offers a different narrative. His idea was to take the best parts of the modern theories of community and recreate a space that could rise above the racial exploitation that existed in the American system. He incorporated the works of Karl Marx and Mahatma Gandhi in relation to non-violence, as well as referencing the proficiency of the Black Church: "This places King's work in a contemporary framework which recognizes his value to scholars and activists who seek to redress social and economic inequality" (Inwood 2009, 489).

Using King's work as a foundation while acknowledging that the importance of community continues to rise, sociologists, theologians, and grassroots organizers have vetted the definition of community over time; thus it is constantly changing. Communities are recognized as critical predictors and indicators of social change as well as fundamental pieces of both capitalist and political economies. They are the results of both internal and external factors and understanding how all of those factors work together is critical (Inwood 2009, 492).

It has been argued by scholars that historically, the difference between the African American communities and white communities is the function of the idea of the individual. African American communities historically have been built around the idea of a collective identity, where the importance that is placed on the well-being of the community as a whole is at least equal to that of the individual members. In this manner, when the individual succeeds, so does the community and vice versa. This view of community differs from the common versions of community that are of a more neoliberal fashion and tend to control urban policy (Inwood 2009, 492).

Herbert notes, "The normative understanding subscribes to a belief in liberal individualism in which success is measured by individual achievement and goals. Critically, this normative vision of community ties into notions of individual responsibility and is a regnant focus of neoliberal governance" (Herbert 2005, 851). The normative concept of community is deployed to "responsible citizens" and facilitated in the "off-load[ing]" of responsibility of well-being to individuals in the guise" of a "community-based approach" (Staheli 2008, 8). In this neoliberal framework, normative visions of the community rely on the understanding of community to "solve problems and to integrate marginalized groups" while disinvesting the state from a traditional focus on "well-being and social justice" (Inwood 2009, 492).

The negative effects of this have been intensely felt by marginalized communities. When viewed in the neoliberal context, the importance of King's work becomes even more obvious. His concept of the Beloved Community encourages a fresh understanding of the community that is necessary for the development of a society that is more equitable. By using his concept, it is possible to combat the conversations about community and urban governance and refocus efforts on social justice (Inwood 2009, 493).

Beloved Community

At the origin of the Beloved Community is the idea that a community is a place where there is a mutual connectedness and respect among all members. The power of love is able to overcome many obstacles. After becoming aware of the Supreme Court victory that disallowed segregated busses, King said:

> [t]he end [of the Civil Rights Movement] is reconciliation; the end is redemption; the end is the creation of the Beloved Community. It is this type of spirit and this type of love that can transform opposers into friends. It is this type of under-standing goodwill that will transform the deep gloom of the old age into the exuberant gladness of the new age. It is this love which will bring about miracles in the hearts of men (King 1956 as quoted on the King Center for Non-Violent Change website: http://www.thekingcenter.org/prog/bc/index.html). (Inwood 2009, 493).

King drew strength from his Christian faith, and this is from where his belief in the power of "love" and its foundation for the Beloved Community stemmed. After helping to found the Southern Christian Leadership Conference, he wrote the following:

> In speaking of love we are not referring to some sentimental emotion. It would be nonsense to urge men to love their op-pressors in an affectionate sense . . . [Instead] there are three words for love in the Greek New Testament. First, there is *Eros*. In Platonic philosophy *Eros* meant the yearning of the soul for the realm of the divine. It has come now to mean a sort of romantic love. Second, there is Philia. It meant intimate

affectionateness towards friends ... When we speak of loving those who oppose us we refer neither to Eros or Philia; we speak of a love which is expressed in the Greek word *Agape*. Agape means nothing sentimental or affectionate; it means understanding, redeeming goodwill for all men, an overflowing love which seeks nothing in return (King 1986b: 8). (Inwood 2009, 493)

King made an important connection between love and community, in a speech titled "America's Chief Moral Dilemma," when he spoke at the University of California at Berkeley in 1967. He defined Agape love as the kind of love that required a person to self-advocate and make it known to oppressors that their actions were wrong. King established an essential link between love and community, bringing together the more Western notions about love and joining them with the African American ideas of community and the human connections that are so vital. King went on to explain that:

Agape is a willingness to go to any length to restore community ... Therefore if I respond to hate with a reciprocal hate I do nothing but intensify the cleavage of a broken community. I can only close the gap in a broken community by meeting hate with love ... In the final analysis, Agape means recognition that all life is interrelated (King 1986d:20). (Inwood 2009, 494)

Drawing on his background as a Baptist minister, King used the concept of Agape love and paralleled it with the community connectedness that was so common in African American communities. It was the belief of the Black Church that the resources of society were meant to be equally shared by all people, creating a foundation of love that brought people together regardless of skin color or economic status (Inwood 2009, 494).

King believed that Jim Crow segregation dehumanized both whites and African Americans. Where the white society used violence and oppression to respond to African American's claims to basic rights, African Americans were forced to live in conditions that were both degrading and inhumane.

In this context, King's concept of Agape love stood as a uniting power, making it possible to build the organization and erect space and place. Here, King uncovered a community model where the main goal was to assign value to the human personality and the relationships born from them. In a speech given in 1957, King clarified that when there is nonviolent resolution grounded in Agape love, the results are redemption and reconciliation. In contrast, violent resolutions lead to emptiness and bitterness. Agape love is the fundamental principle upon which the society that King proposed was built upon (Inwood 2009, 495).

It was King's proposal that in addition to a renovation of US society, there also needed to be new communities created, built upon a foundation of Agape love. King was able to combine African American Christian opinions on love and community with the non-violent ideals of Gandhi and fully investigate the driving causes of racism and class inequality. He was then able to transfer those findings and utilize them to formulate a vision for a society unplagued by racism and economic injustice. King articulated his discontent with US society in his address before the Southern Christian Leadership Conference titled, "*Where Do We Go From Here?*" It was here that he stated that the US society was one that:

will keep people in slavery for 244 years, will "thingify" them—make them things. Therefore they will exploit them, and poor people generally, economically. And a nation that will exploit economically will have to have foreign investments and everything else, and will have to use its military to protect them. All of these problems are tied together (King 1986e:251). (Inwood 2009, 495)

Dr. King recognized the way that so many factors were interrelated, creating the dynamic that allowed economic, racial, and social oppression to be connected in spite of time and physical distance. The difficulties experienced by African Americans connect to social justice. There is also a connection between US intervention abroad and the mistreatment of poor people in the US. King also recognized that there was a connection between anti-colonial politics and the development of African American political culture that dates as far back as the early twentieth century (Inwood 2009, 495).

In his book *Where Do We Go From Here? Chaos or Community*, in a chapter titled "The World House," King espoused that "self-preservation as the first law of life" is one of the basic values of a traditional capitalist society (King 2010 [1967], 177). It was his desire to shift the mindset of society and make the recognition of everyone who labored for the success of the Western nations first and foremost. King elaborated on this by saying:

We are lasting debtors to known and unknown men and women. When we arise in the morning, we go to the bathroom where we reach for a sponge which is provided for us by a pacific islander. We reach for soap that is created for us by a European. Then at the table we drink coffee which is provided us by a South American, or tea by a Chinese or cocoa by a West African. Before we leave for our jobs we are already beholden to more than half the world (Inwood 2009, 496).

The neoliberal economic process is a component of daily life that abuses the talents of the poor. By globalizing economic processes, the way is paved for an existence where the well-off population becomes blind to the insufficiency that surrounds them (Inwood 2009, 496).

In order for the Beloved Community to become a reality, King prescribed a situation where wealthy nations made a commitment to provide economic assistance to areas that were underdeveloped. He believed that those nations were morally obligated to provide that assistance, but at the same time were not given the freedom to control those nations which they were assisting. With a common goal of abolishing poverty, disease, and ignorance through the use of compassion and commitment, a foreign aid program would be successful (Inwood 2009, 496).

In order to create the type of society that King envisioned, there would need to be a transfer from a society that was materialistic to a society that focused on people and creation. The advantages of both capitalism and socialism would need to be combined in order to achieve this type of society. In his words:

[t]hat capitalism has often left a gulf between superfluous wealth taken from the many to give luxuries to the few and has encouraged small-hearted men to become cold and conscienceless . . . The profit motive, when it is the sole basis of an economic system, encourages a cutthroat competition and selfish ambition that inspire men to be more I centered than thou centered (King 1967:186). (Inwood 2009, 496)

"In this passage, King criticized capitalism for creating a society devoid of the kind of community connections he advocated for in the Beloved Community and is the antithesis of Agape love and community connectedness" (Inwood 2009, 497).

King proposed a new economic tradition combining traditions of the African American Church with elements of Marx and western capitalism. King wrote in 1967, "the good and just society is neither the thesis of capitalism nor the antithesis of Communism, but a socially conscious democracy which reconciles the truths of individualism and collectivism" (King 2010 [1967], 187). This economic tradition is what King called the Beloved Community. It is the ideal compilation of the best of the African American and Western viewpoints of social and economic justice. King envisioned a place that denounced poverty and racism and brought the individual's identity into the collective community identity. Political and economic powers must coexist in order to bring this community to life. Geographic spaces have to be repositioned and redefined, and for this to occur there has to be a common belief that a community that is grounded in love can ultimately bring about a positive change in society (Inwood 2009, 498).

Ultimately, King dreamed of a society that realized the importance of people reaching their potential and did not turn to hate and exploitation as methods of solving problems. In this society, the needs of the poor are acknowledged and addressed, and the identities, strengths, and contributions of individuals are valued within the larger community context. King's idea of Beloved Community embraces differences and advocates for "each of us claiming the identities and cultural legacies that shape who we are and how we live in the world" (Inwood 2009, 499). By focusing on redistributing wealth and privilege in the US, he felt the US could lead the world in making a shift to that way of thinking. It was King's belief that the only thing standing in the way of America paying an adequate wage to every American citizen was a lack of social vision. A program that guarantees this is necessary in order to establish the Beloved Community. By providing for the poor, it would be possible to establish a level of economic security for all people. Dr. King had multiple theories on how to improve the current capitalist geographic order and linked his theories and messages to issues being addressed worldwide:

> Everywhere in Latin America one finds a tremendous resentment of the United States, and the resentment is always strongest among the poor and the darker peoples of the continents. The life and destiny of Latin America are in the hands of United States Corporations … Here we see racism in its more sophisticated form: neocolonialism . . . In recent years their countries [referring to Africa, Asia and Latin America] have been invaded by automobiles, Coca-Cola, and Hollywood so that even remote villages have become aware of the wonders and blessings available to God's white children (Inwood 2009, 499).

Dr. King boldly spoke out about US domination around the world. Shortly before his murder, he spoke about the need for the US to develop a more cohesive relationship with the less developed people of the world. His concept of the Beloved Community was how he proposed to do this. This concept encourages people to come together both literally and figuratively, building upon a foundation of love and non-violence (Inwood 2009, 500).

A Way Out of No Way

Repeatedly throughout his writings, sermons, and speeches, King asserted the need for an Economic Bill of Rights that, according to economist and public theologian Michael Greene, would "promote and protect human dignity, recognize our interrelatedness, and contribute to the restoration of community" (Greene 2014, 36). It was his belief that because humans were created by God, they were afforded certain God-given rights. This included civil, political, and economic rights. In order to ensure that all people were afforded a significant measure of human dignity, it was critical that those rights be recognized as equal pieces of a complete package, none being more important than another. It was King's belief that it was only when the rights were recognized collectively that human dignity would be protected and community could be restored: "If economic rights, including the right to a job, are missing from the picture, King contends, we merely 'exist'" (Greene 2014, 37).

With the ultimate goal being to rise above mere existence, King called for full employment and income support for those that were not able or expected to work.

For King, this supplementation of the political with an Economic Bill of Rights is central to the broadening of democracy and part of the requisite foundational underpinning of a blessed community that respects and promotes human dignity (Greene 2014, 38).

King's vision for a Beloved Community was a place where everyone was able to live with dignity and a modicum of self-worth as they lived out their potential and contributed to the success of the community as a whole. It was his belief that it was "unrealistic to expect individuals to shoulder the enormous burden of eradicating poverty and joblessness" (Greene 2014, 39).

King believed that there was a need for both an employment and income guarantee. An employment guarantee meant that every person had the right to hold a job that paid a livable wage. An income guarantee meant that even those individuals who were unable to fully participate in the paid workforce would still be able to access a standard of living that afforded them basic human dignity. It was King's belief that these two provisions existed in a joint fashion rather than singularly. At the foundation of the Beloved Community is the collaboration between social and economic justice and genuine full employment. Guaranteed wages must be partnered with guaranteed jobs. Every person capable of working should be working. For people who work these jobs, there is a "guaranteed annual wage as minimum income for every American family, so that there is an economic floor, and nobody falls beneath that" (Greene 2014, 41).

Also, in this Economic Bill of Rights is a departure from the school of thought that job training must be emphasized above and before the procuring of full employment. While it is important to have the necessary training in order to perform a job, focusing only on training implies that the jobless possess inferiorities that must be addressed or even "fixed" before they can become employable members of the community. King's principle in the Beloved Community was "jobs first, training later" (Greene 2014, 42). By assessing the needs of the community and seeing the gaps and places where work needs to be done, we can create jobs to utilize the skill sets of the jobless, thereby providing a means by which they can earn their minimum annual wage.

CHAPTER 12

FACTORS CONTRIBUTING TO POVERTY

When there is an unevenness in the geography in terms of economics, there is spatial inequality – disparity that exists due to location. In the last few decades, especially in the times leading up to the COVID-19 Pandemic, these disparities have become more obvious (Fikri, Newman, and O'dell 2021, 3).

The fates of American families are closely tied with that of their communities, which makes domestic policies that are place-centered, naturally people-centered as well. The foundational ideas of equity in space and race are very similar. It is for these reasons that it is imperative that the current presidential administration, alongside Congress, address the issue of spatial inequality when looking at domestic policy. They have high hopes of using their time in our history to "build back better," and their domestic policy agenda must reflect that with racial equity and spatial equity on the agenda (Fikri, Newman, and O'dell 2021, 5). This transfer from policymaking that is spatially uncertain to that which pays specific attention to geography, will entail a government structure that is focused on inclusivity. The goal is to make regional inclusive growth a priority, and this will have to extend beyond a single program (Fikri, Newman, and O'dell 2021, 6). Across the nation, all communities would see benefits from an "elevated, empowered, centralized entity to drive federal economic development policy" (Fikri, Newman, and O'dell 2021, 8).

No matter what structure is utilized, it must be somehow aligned with or be an extension of the Economic Development Administration (EDA). The EDA, which focuses solely on domestic economic development, is the only government agency of its kind. Small in size, this agency would benefit from an increased budget to assist it in meeting the needs of long-term economic development challenges that the country faces. It would take the influence of Congress and executive leaders to make the kind of changes necessary to improve the agency's functioning (Fikri, Newman, and O'dell 2021, 8). Moreover, "The Biden administration should focus on empowering the EDA to serve more of a strategic and centralized, coordinating role for relevant activities. An empowered EDA must provide coherence, leadership, vision, and final accountability for economic development policies across the bureaucracy" (Fikri, Newman, and O'dell 2021, 9).

In order to facilitate this change, federal policymakers need to reevaluate the instruments that are available for addressing economic development finance and consider incorporating pieces from models on international development. Particular attention should be given to the encouragement of activity from the private sector to those areas that are consistently falling behind:

Here the new U.S. Development Finance Corporation (DFC), successor to the Overseas Private Investment Corporation (OPIC), could serve as a model. The DFC is designed to provide the sort of financing private markets will not—loan guarantees, direct equity contributions, and securitization across high-risk entrepreneurs or locations—that allow private commerce to take hold and flourish. A Domestic DFC (DDFC) might join with EDA in such an approach to incubate market activity in some of the country's weakest-market areas where private investors fear to tread, from the rural Deep South and the tribal West to distressed urban corners of the Northeast or Midwest. Such vitally important financial instruments are currently missing in the space between EDA grants, SBA loans, and CDFI Fund allocations. (Fikri, Newman, and O'dell 2021,8)

In order to include spatial consideration within economic policy-making, there must be a strong legislative agenda that is focused on stimulating growth. Any proposed solutions must have the resources necessary to accommodate both neighborhoods and larger regions, as well as tactics that will be able to address the construction of success on multiple economic fronts (Fikri, Newman, and O'dell 2021,11).

All places need to have an equal chance at experiencing prosperity and being competitive in the modern economy if spatial inequality is going to be combated. This will require the federal government to provide the necessary tools to provide access to markets in order to disperse the benefits of economic growth. Policymakers need to look past the common behaviors of allowing places with low or disadvantaged populations to be left out of awards and investments because of a belief that the impact would be too small. The lack of local partners who are capable of providing assistance, can no longer be grounds for omission from assistance; instead, these places need to be targeted from the onset of development (Fikri, Newman, and O'dell 2021, 12).

One of the largest disparities between the parts of the country that are flourishing and those that are struggling are the working people. They are also the foundation of community wealth. For example, "One-fifth of the adult residents of economically distressed zip codes have not completed high school on average, compared to one out of every 20 in prosperous zip codes" (Fikri, Newman, and O'dell 2021, 14).

How States Can Help

Research shows that Americans who grow up in areas wrought with economic distress are subjected to a myriad of other disadvantages, including but not limited to low-performing schools, higher crime rates, and health and environmental hazards. As I mentioned, the coronavirus pandemic has exacerbated these disparities, with low-income neighborhoods and those housing racial and ethnic minorities being hit especially hard ("How States Can Direct Economic Development to Places and People in Need", 1).

In efforts to assist struggling areas, billions of dollars have been funneled into "place-based" economic development programs over the last four decades with lofty goals of creating more jobs and increasing property values in targeted locations. These programs include community-development block grants, low-income housing tax credits and new markets tax credits. Unfortunately, research has shown that these programs tend to end up helping wealthy locations instead of the disadvantaged locations that were targeted, and when they do reach the intended locations, they are not actually the correct assistance that is needed ("How States Can Direct Economic Development to Places and People in Need", 1).

According to the Pew Charitable Trusts' analysis of these "place-based" assistance programs, states should do the following in order to begin resolving these issues:

- Target programs using quantitative measures.
- Systematically assess geographic targeting.
- Regularly update the set of eligible locations.
- Tailor economic development strategies to local needs.
- Create job opportunities for low-income residents. ("How States Can Direct Economic Development to Places and People in Need", 1).

State policymakers have the primary responsibility of determining where programs are available, and this gives them the power to begin solving this problem. In order to do this effectively, they need improved data and analysis pertaining to where place-based programs are used as well as who benefits from them. Efforts need to be refocused, paying particular attention to the way that place-based financial incentives make the expansion of economic opportunities for struggling families in struggling places the priority ("How States Can Direct Economic Development to Places and People in Need", 13).

Opportunity Theory

Opportunity theory is the notion that people are motivated and driven by the opportunities that are available to them. According to this theory, people who are poor desire to achieve the same things as other people in society. The difference is that the likelihood of poor people fulfilling those desires by methods deemed acceptable by society is not as high as the likelihood of their non-poor peers. Opportunity theory says that people from low socio-economic backgrounds with few opportunities for success use whatever opportunities may arise to achieve the desired success. In other words, their social situation often dictates paths to success. For example, a teen living in a poor neighborhood who wants to experience the middle-class lifestyle depicted in the media may turn to selling drugs in order to fund that lifestyle because that is what is readily available in his social situation (Copeland 1994, 152).

Scholars Lisbeth Schorr and Frances Fox Piven have differing views on the opportunity theory. According to Schorr, poor people can achieve success when they have adequate support. She believes that positive support leads to the development of a positive sense of self. According to Piven, poor people can have the same opportunities to succeed as the rest of the population if the economic and social system is altered to reflect the thinking that poor people are poor because they don't have money and not because they are unmotivated or value deficient. Poor people do not need to be changed, rather there needs to be a change in society (Copeland 1994, 152).

CHAPTER 13

WHERE WE ARE TODAY

Poverty is a result of systemic racism that has plagued our country and communities of color from the beginning. Throughout the years, national and local government, as well as banks, have played a role in helping to keep people in poverty, especially people of color. This is why, arguably, there are wide disparities in wealth, health, housing and education.

Poverty in the United States is defined by Merriam Webster as "the state of one who lacks a usual or socially acceptable amount of money or material possessions." However, it should be noted that the United States does not truly define poverty; it measures poverty. Poverty means more than an absence or lack of resources. Because of this factor, it will take more than donations and handouts to completely eradicate the problem. This is one reason that it is so important to restructure the approach used when tackling poverty.

Based on the U.S. Census Bureau's 2017 estimate, the poverty rate was 12.3 percent. That number equates to approximately 39.7 million Americans living in poverty according to the official measure, which was developed in the 1960s alongside Lyndon B. Johnson's War on Poverty. The supplemental poverty measure rate was slightly higher, at 13.9 percent. Currently, the official measure is based on data obtained from the Current Population Survey Annual Social and Economic Supplement. This is a survey that is sent to households in the United

States, which means that homeless, military, and incarcerated individuals are not accounted for.

The official poverty measure accounts for the cost of a minimum food diet based on family size, composition, and the age of the householder. Any person living in a household where the income is below their relative poverty threshold (as determined by the U.S. Census Bureau), is considered to be living in poverty. The supplemental measure of poverty is slightly more complex and accounts for basic living costs which are variable depending on the state of residency. Since the launch of the War on Poverty programs after 1964, the poverty rate has varied between 11 and 15 percent ("What Is the Current Poverty Rate in the United States? - UC Davis Center for Poverty Research" 2012).

CHAPTER 14

WHAT'S NEXT

We cannot ignore the adverse effects gentrification has had on communities of color over generations. Both public and private leaders have the opportunity and the ability to put into place strategies that can afford opportunities for long-time residents to benefit from increased investment in their communities, and they can be a part of some of the changes taking place as well. In order to prevent displacement, there is a need for the protection of residents, more affordable housing, and the preservation of existing affordable housing ("Gentrification Explained | Urban Displacement Project" 2017).

Since the government continues to neglect to make poverty a true public conversation accompanied by action, we can no longer look for solutions from a system that has created this situation from the beginning. We need real solutions, because half of our neighborhoods are missing due to systemic racism and poverty. This phraseology comes from something that Eugene "Gus"Newport wrote in a 2004 article for the *New England Journal of Public Policy*. As he expounded on his work of serving as Director of the Dudley Street Neighborhood Initiative in Boston, he recalled a site visit to a neighborhood non-profit where one of the trustees looked at a map of a blighted community and inquired about "dark spaces." It was soon revealed that these dark spaces were abandoned lots. Newport writes that the trustee responded: "We come out here to award a grant to replace some worn furniture when half of the neighborhood is missing" (Newport 2004). In other words, a significant amount of people were displaced, gone, and no longer living in the community because of disinvestment in the area and the people.

To give you some perspective on how Gus has influenced and inspired my work, as well as a generation of sociologists, community leaders and civil rights activists, it is important to know that he was mentored by Malcolm X and Adam Clayton Powell, Jr. Here are some notable highlights from his storied career over the last sixty years or so. During the 1960s, he chaired The Monroe County Non-Partisan Political League, the largest civil rights organization in Rochester, NY. He served the city of Berkeley, CA as a two-term Mayor from 1979-1986. Newport served as the vice-president from the United States to the World Peace Council in the 1980s. Additionally, he is the former director of the Institute of Community Economics and in 2005, he served on the five-person advisory body that oversaw the planning to rebuild New Orleans following the devastation and displacements of thousands of people in the aftermath of Hurricane Katrina.

It is not enough to invest and give to financial institutions when there is clear evidence that they have conspired with the system that we now find ourselves fighting against. The COVID-19 Pandemic has clearly and fully uncovered the racial disparities and economic wealth divides caused by an unjust system that has purposely created laws and policies that have kept people from getting ahead and flourishing.

We need people with moral courage to fight for the poor. We don't need more programs; we need real solutions. Martin Luther King, Jr. gave us a prescription and a blueprint in 1964 for abolishing poverty before he was assassinated four years later. King stated:

Underneath the invitation to prepare programs is the premise that the government is inherently benevolent - it only awaits presentation of imaginative ideas. When these issues arise from fertile minds, they will be accepted, enacted, and implemented. This premise shifts the burden of responsibility from the white majority, by pretending it is withholding nothing, and places it on the oppressed minority, by pretending the latter is asking for nothing. This is a fable, not a fact. Neither the government nor any government that has sanctioned a century of denial can be depicted as ardent and impatient to bestow gifts of freedom (King 2010 [1967], 144).

He goes on to explain that there is no point in making plans to build a home if we do not have the money necessary or the ability to garner the land needed. To do so would be acting out of logical order (King 2010 [1967], 144). King went on to explicitly state that there was only one idea worth examining and that was the idea of eliminating poverty completely on a national scale (King 2010 [1967], 170).

According to King, there was a simple solution. By enacting a guaranteed income, poverty could be eliminated directly. It was his belief that if poverty was eliminated, there would be a direct effect on housing and education. People would become purchasers, bettering their housing situations. When these people begin to feel a sense of economic security, positive psychological changes would be inevitable. As they grew in control of their own lives and decisions, they would become more confident in their abilities to actualize self-improvements.

In order for this system of guaranteed income to be successful, there would have to be two conditions. The guaranteed income must be based on the median income of society and not the lowest levels.

A guaranteed income at the lowest level would only guarantee a stag-nate existence in poverty conditions. Second, the guaranteed income must remain proportionate to the social income, rising as it does. This proposal of guaranteed income was not a civil rights program. Instead, it was a program that would benefit all of the poor, including those who were white and made up the majority (King 2010 [1967], 173).

Because we failed to hear King then, it has to become an imme-diate community effort if we are going to stop this vicious cycle. The federal government has tried, but offering programs is not enough. The community can pressure state and local governments to do the right thing.

We have seen this more recently after the assassination in 2020 of George Floyd, an unarmed Black man in Minneapolis who died after a police officer held his knee on the 46-year-old's neck for more than nine minutes. In the aftermath of his murder, a nationwide pro-test spilled across cities large and small. Community organizing and clearly defined goals and demands ushered in measured change. This evidences that when people come together for the common good, the community can exact change. Take my home state, Mississippi, for example. I would have never thought that in my lifetime I would see the confederate flag come down. However, because people on the local and state level stood up and demanded change, the flag came down. We also need people who have platforms to take a stand. Again, in Mississippi, there was a person who had the courage to use his plat-form to help push this fight.

His name is Kylin Hill; he is from my hometown of Columbus, and we played high school football for the same alma mater. He now plays for Mississippi State University. This young man had a lot to lose, being one of the top-rated players in the country. However, he used his platform and said if the flag didn't come down, he would not be playing for the state of Mississippi. This is the kind of action that is needed on the state and local level if we are ever going to change our communities. We have seen situations like this across the country on state and local levels. We have also seen corporate companies investing and giving back. Although we don't know what the results will be or if that money will ever reach the people it was intended to reach, we do know now that collectively we can demand change. This is why poverty must be front and center in the fight for equality.

If we are to redeem the soul of this nation, we must be the catalyst for change in our communities. This means we need a new, out-of-the-box approach to this age-old problem.

First, we must recognize that poverty is still a problem. Second, we must change the theology of those who are influencers and decision-makers in our communities. Third, we have to empower people in our communities. Fourth, we have to create new models that will transform our communities.

All of this is crystallized in what Gus Newport calls "Good Governance." Good governance is evident when people who are in charge engage in meaningful dialogue about what matters, with the people who will be affected by public policy. There is a constant flow of research and analysis of policies and approaches as situations and circumstances change. Strategies employed must change as the conditions and needs of the people change (Newport 2004). Times are changing, and our approaches need to change too. Upon his passing, US Congressman and civil rights humanitarian John Lewis, left us with the following words:

> You filled me with hope about the next chapter of the great American story when you used your power to make a difference in our society. Millions of people

motivated simply by human compassion laid down the burdens of division. Around the country and the world, you set aside race, class, age, language, and nationality to demand respect for human dignity (Lewis, 2020).

This is what it looks like when we take a new approach to an old problem.

Martin Luther King, Jr. said when we tolerate injustice, we are complicit. He said we have a moral obligation to stand up, speak up and speak out. He said that democracy is an act, and each generation is responsible for doing its part to help build a nation and society that is at peace with itself. He said we have to learn the lessons from history, because for centuries before us people have struggled. He said that the truths from the past can help us find solutions in the present. He said we must use global movements to unite and stop profiting from the exploitation of others (Lewis, 2020).

This is our charge, our challenge that we have been called to take on. We must be willing to stand up and speak out.

When historians pick up their pens to write the story of the 21st century, let them say that it was your generation who laid down the heavy burdens of hate at last and that peace finally triumphed over violence, aggression, and war. So, I say to you, walk with the wind, brothers and sisters, and let the spirit of peace and the power of everlasting love be your guide. (Lewis, 2020)

We must learn from those who fought before us and use that knowledge to change the future.

CHAPTER 15

WHAT WE CAN DO TO CREATE 6 MILLION JOBS AND 1.4 MILLION BUSINESSES

What is the "Black Tax"? In his book, *The Black Tax: The Cost of Being Black in America,* Shawn D. Rochester refers to what he calls the Black Tax, as "the cost of implicit bias on African Americans" (Rochester 2017, 4). While the moral implications of the Black Tax on the African American community are large, the financial impacts are even larger. The African American community does not lack the desire to leave a legacy, however this Black Tax creates a seemingly insurmountable gap between desire and ability. Research supports the presence of what is known as the 2% Rule. Throughout history, Black Americans have been restricted to 2% levels in various areas that contribute to the accumulation of wealth, including the economy, politics, and society as a whole. Some examples of the situations faced by Black Americans historically are:

- Black Americans were emancipated but denied land, capital, credit, fair wages, means of production, skill development and free trade (all of which were far below the 2% level).
- Black American held less than 2% of U.S. wealth for 250 years.
- Black Americans owned less than 2% of all U.S. land for over 400 years (currently 1%).
- Black Americans held less than 2% of almost all high-skilled, high-paying jobs in all industries for 150 years after emancipation.

- Black Americans received less than 2% of the $120 billion distributed to Americans via federal housing subsidies.
- Less than 2% of the adult Black population was allowed to attain college degrees as of 1950. (Rochester 2017, 89)

Presently, this trend has carried over and permeated the interactions that Black Americans have with each other, perpetuating the cycle and affecting their economics. Today, Black Americans:

- Spend less than 2% of their combined $1.2 trillion income on Black enterprises.
- Deposit less than 2% of their combined $130 billion of deposits in Black banks.
- Spend less than 2% of their combined $1.2 trillion on education. (Rochester 2017, 90)

These actions negatively impact the creation of jobs and the development of businesses. Black enterprises have unknowingly imposed a second tax on themselves by not pouring their resources back into their own businesses and banks. This ultimately leads to lower incomes for both Black consumers and enterprises. This 2% phenomenon is also present today in many companies as evidenced by the following:

- Black-owned small businesses received less than 2% (1.7%) of all loan money distributed through the SBA, according to an analysis by the *Wall Street Journal*.
- Less than 2% (1%) of tech companies with Black founders receive venture capital funding. (FastCoexist.com)
- Less than 2% (1%) of Fortune 500 CEOs are Black.
- Blacks only make up about 2% of recent hires at tech firms. (*The Atlantic magazine*)
- Less than 2% of schoolteachers and administrators nationwide are Black men.

- HBCUs (Historically Black Colleges and Universities) received less than 2% of the more than $140 billion in federal grants for science and engineering awarded in the 1990s.
- Blacks consume more media per person than any other group, yet less than 2% (1%) of film executives are directors who are members of the Academy of Motion Picture Arts and Sciences are Black.
- Black women make up less than 2% of all lawyers in the United States.
- Black men make up less than 2% of all lawyers in the United States.
- Blacks make up 1% to 2% of all financial advisors.
- Less than 2% of all U.S. farms are Black-owned. (Rochester 2017, 91-93)

The combination of past and present discriminations and un-derrepresentation in careers and industries has severely impeded the ability of Black Americans to accumulate wealth.

In order to combat the adverse effects and increase the employment levels and business development within the Black community, Rochester suggests a combination of strategies that must be employed: there needs to be higher rates of inclusion of African Americans in supplier programs, safer communities with embedded economic opportunities, higher post-secondary education levels, and action from both the government and private sectors (Rochester 2017, 98-99).

Rochester suggests using two new models as the foundation for the facilitation of this change: SOuL, and PHD. SOuL, an acronym meaning Stewardship, Ownership, and Legacy, focuses on individuals effectively managing their personal and household finances in a manner that allows them to accumulate wealth that will be able to be passed onto future generations (Rochester 2017, 99). PHD is an acronym for Purchase, Hire and Deposit. In order to bolster economic development within the African American community, there must be an increased focus on purchasing products and utilizing services from Black enterprises, hiring Black Americans to work well-paying jobs, and depositing funds back into Black financial institutions (Rochester 2017, 100). This formula will create a situation where the wealth remains within the community: "Getting your PHD is about facilitating trade and commerce with Black employees, business-es, and financial institutions to create a solid foundation for wealth accumulation" (Rochester 2017, 100). African Americans have to be an integral part of all aspects of the economic community in order for them to be a help instead of a hindrance.

If we follow the PHD formula, the impact of the Black tax can be lessened. It will be possible to create an environment that cultivates the closing of the massive job and business gap in the Black commu-nity, working towards creating those 6 million jobs that are needed (Rochester 2017, 100).

Purchasing is like a chain, with the links being consumers, busi-nesses, and governments purchasing services and products from Black businesses. In order to create jobs and businesses within the Black community, it is imperative that each link of the chain makes it a priority to purchase goods and services from Black businesses, as well as encourage others to do the same. The more that is purchased, the higher that the demand becomes, and the demand for those goods and services creates the need for more employees and businesses to provide those products and services. This is the job creation that is so desperately needed.

Black consumers have a purchasing power of $1.2 trillion. What is not so commonly known is the fact that this same purchasing power supports 24 million jobs in the economy. The main problem with these facts is that the majority of that economic impact (job creation and business development) occurs outside of the Black community (Rochester 2017, 103). By keeping more of this economic activity within the Black community it would be possible to close that employment gap: "Since Black enterprises currently employ almost 1 million people, and Black representation in corporate and government supply chains is so low, even a small increase in demand could generate the need for 1 million to 2 million additional jobs" (Rochester 2017, 104), raising the total jobs to that 6 million mark.

Planning for a future that is sustainable requires a community that is willing to compromise on specific needs that have to be addressed in the present, how addressing those needs will affect the future people and conditions, and what type of accommodations they are willing to make in order to plan for the best possible outcomes. This may require some adjustments to present lifestyles of the community, and these adjustments have to be accepted by the present members of the community as well as align with their values, while also not jeopardizing the opportunities of the future generations. Sustainability requires the community to distinguish between essentials and desires and come to a common understanding of what is enough. This collective and mutual understanding will allow for a clearer vision of how to adjust the present to provide for a better future (Flint 2013, 4).

A community is built when there is an assembling of people who grow to trust and depend on both each other and the land which they inhabit. As the people change, the landscape changes and vice versa. These changes are in part due to the evolving relationships present in the community. The shared identity of the community, which is "grounded in its history, which must be passed from one generation to the next if the community is to know itself throughout the passage of time" (Flint 2013, 5). King's vision for a Beloved Community was a place where everyone was able to live with dignity and a modicum of self-worth as they lived out their potential and contributed to the success of the community as a whole. (Greene 2014, 39)

The examples of the Dudley Street Neighborhood Initiative and Mission Waco can be seen as blueprints to implement long-lasting sustainable "beloved" communities. I refer to these communities as sustainable "beloved" communities because you have to have a theology rooted in love in order to achieve this concept of sustainable "beloved" community. This concept will require sustainable "beloved" development because planned development is not always a community. In this development process, you must have the right person/people to bring about the right approach. Churches, communities, and community leaders can lead this development process with developers and local governments to bring real change to their communities. At the end of the day, when communities speak for themselves, they have the power to demand change.

What I have found in my research is that it is possible to overcome gentrification and poverty using the models of DSNI and Mission Waco. Both models are examples of sustainable "beloved" communities who have made it their mission to approach their communities in a holistic way. Gentrification doesn't have to be a narrative of poor people getting pushed out of communities.

Both DSNI and Mission Waco have done important work at a local level. However, there are still working people in these communities who struggle with the reality of poverty every day.

If we are to achieve King's full prescription of Beloved Community, we have to consider the national vision he proposed in 1967 in his book, *Where Do We Go From Here: Chaos or Community?* King wanted guaranteed income and one of the ways that he wanted to guarantee this income was for the federal government to provide this guaranteed income. The time has come for all of us to pressure the president, vice president, senators, congressional representatives, and everyone who represents us on the local, state and national levels to promote an Economic Bill of Rights.

CONCLUSION

There is a need to abolish poverty. Just as the abolition of slavery was accomplished by a constitutional amendment, the same needs to be done with poverty. As Dr. Martin Luther King, Jr. said, "The curse of poverty has no justification in our age. The time has come for us to civilize ourselves by the total, direct and immediate abolition of poverty" (2010 [1967], 175).

There needs to be a constitutional amendment that codifies there will be no poverty. The Constitution was amended to guarantee the right to vote with the 15th amendment and abolished slavery with the 13th amendment. Poverty still exists because it has yet to be abolished. There is a need for an Economic Bill of Rights that provides a guaranteed income in order to abolish poverty. "From a variety of different directions, the strands are drawing together for a contemporary social and Economic Bill of Rights to supplement the Constitution's Political Bill of Rights" (King 2010 [1967], 211).

The COVID-19 Pandemic has proven that America has the bandwidth to abolish poverty. The government has already sent three rounds of stimulus checks and gave adults with children an up-front child tax credit for a whole year. We need to send out more stimulus checks, and the stimulus checks need to be larger amounts. The checks need to be large enough and continue until the people who are receiving those checks are no longer poor. This is what King had in mind; it is direct.

This is not nine-months-of-job-training-at-the-community-college-followed-by-an-interview-to-get-an-entry-level-job-at-minimum-wage-and-hope-you-can-work-your-way-up-over-the-course-of-five-years kind of change. This will abolish poverty now, directly and immediately. This is what King was aiming for. It was possible then and it is possible now. We are living in a particular moment in history where we have been given the unique opportunity to give everyone an opportunity. The COVID-19 Pandemic is the mirror America needed to look in so that America can fix what it has broken.

If we abolish poverty by creating jobs that pay living wages, take care of those who cannot work, expand our theology and rethink how we develop communities, then we can marshal our efforts to ensure that we maintain and sustain those residents who make up the DNA of the community. If poor people are not displaced from their communities in the process of gentrification, we can end the narrative of poor people being pushed out or displaced.

Gentrification with Justice

In order to restore health to our neighborhoods, we need gentrification that has a positive undertone and does not seek to displace the citizens that are disadvantaged. People who possess vision, compassion, and business insight are needed. They need to use their knowledge and expertise, as well as their business connections, to guarantee that lower-income residents play a key part in restoring their neighborhoods. Those that are landowners need to be motivated by faith and allow their faith to bridge the gaps between relationships and capital (Lupton 2007, 116).

People of the Kingdom have been called to provide for the needs of the less fortunate. This is explicitly explained in Scriptures, and for ages has been a right and a responsibility. In order to partake in the joy that can arise when a city is revitalized, every effort must be made to ensure that everyone, including the poor, is able to be a part of the process (Lupton 2007, 116).

The commandments of loving God and thy neighbor come before the Great Commission. The body of Christ possesses all that it needs to enact justice and the changes desired in the ever-evolving cities. The surface barely has been scratched on the enumerable talents available to be put to work for the Kingdom and biblical justice; "Gifts like deal-making, lending, insuring, lawyering, marketing, architecture, and real estate developing to name a few" (Lupton 2007, 117).

Our communities need an infusion of redeeming values and actions. Those that are best outfitted to provide these infusions are those who hold the belief that their highest calling in life is to love God and their neighbor. We can develop mixed-income housing, give tax incentives to seniors on fixed incomes, and establish loan funds for down-payment assistance. By simply being genuinely good people, it is possible to create an environment where the poor are able to partake of the benefits of a stimulated city and better their own circumstances at the same time. "We can harness the growing tide of gentrification so that it becomes a redemptive force in our cities. In a word, we can bring "gentrification with justice" (Lupton 2007, 117). Gentrification does not equal displacement.

Chapter 1

BIBLIOGRAPHY

Baldwin, Lewis V. 1995. *Toward the Beloved Community: Martin Luther King Jr. and South Africa.* Cleveland, OH: Pilgrim Press.

Bergen, Wesley J. 2014. "The Lectionary as a Guide to Thinking about Poverty." *Theology Today* 70 (4): 417–29. https://doi.org/10.1177/0040573613506731.

Brennan, Mark A. 2015. *Community Leadership Development: A Compendium of Theory, Research, and Application.* Abingdon, Oxon: Routledge. (Kindle)

Brown, Kevin. "My Journey From a Non-Relational God to a Relational God 'Surrendering to Grace, Mercy and Love.'" Interpretation of the Christian Message, Perkins School of Theology, 2014 (15-25).

Brueggemann, Walter. 2001. *The Prophetic Imagination.* Minneapolis: Fortress Press.

Butler, Jonathan Grabinsky and Stuart M. n.d. "The Anti-Poverty Case for 'Smart' Gentrification, Part 1." Brookings. https://www.brookings.edu/blog/social-mobility-memos/2015/02/10/the-anti-poverty-case-for-smart-gentrification-part-1/.

Butler, Jonathan Grabinsky and Stuart M. n.d. "The Anti-Poverty Case for 'Smart' Gentrification, Part 2." Brookings. Accessed February 10, 2021. https://www.brookings.edu/blog/social-mobility-memos/2015/02/11/the-anti-poverty-case-for-smart-gentrification-part-2/.

Carmichael, Stokely [Kwame Ture] and Charles V Hamilton. 1992 [originally 1967]. *Black Power: The Politics of Liberation in America.* New York: Vintage Books.

Clapp, Rodney. 1996. *A Peculiar People: The Church as Culture in a Post-Christian Society*. Downers Grove, IL: Intervarsity Press.

Cone, James H. 1997. *Black Theology and Black Power*. Maryknoll, NY: Orbis Books.

Cone, James H. 2010. *A Black Theology of Liberation*. Maryknoll, NY: Orbis Books.

Copeland, Warren R. 1994. *And the Poor Get Welfare: The Ethics of Poverty in the United States*. Nashville: Abingdon Press, in cooperation with The Churches' Center for Theology and Public Policy, Washington, D.C.

Corbett, Steve, Brian Fikkert, John Perkins, and David Platt. 2014. *When Helping Hurts How to Alleviate Poverty Without Hurting the Poor... and Yourself*. Chicago, IL: Moody Publishers.

Daniels, David D., III. 2019. "Against Poverty: The Holy Spirit and Pentecostal Economic Ministries." Chapter Two (pp. 30-53) in *The Mighty Transformer: The Holy Spirit Advocates for Social Justice*, edited by Antipas L. Harris. Irving, Texas: GIELD Academic Press.

Despard, Michal Grinstein-Weiss, Brinda Gupta, Yung Chun, Hedwig Lee, and Mathieu. 2020. "Housing Hardships Reach Unprecedented Heights during the COVID-19 Pandemic." Brookings. June 1, 2020. https://www.brookings.edu/blog/up-front/2020/06/01/housing-hardships-reach-unprecedented-heights-during-the-covid-19-pandemic/.

"DSNI." n.d. DSNI. Accessed February 1, 2021. https://www.dsni.org.

Du Bois, W. E. B. 2008. [originally 1903] *The Souls of Black Folk*. Edited by Brent Hayes Edwards. Oxford World's Classics. London, England: Oxford University Press.

"Dudley Street Neighborhood Initiative." Community Uprooted: Eminent Domain in the U.S.: Loyola University Chicago. Accessed February 1, 2021. https://www.luc.edu/eminent-domain/siteessays/bostonma/dudleystreetneighborhoodinitiative/.

Emerson, Michael O, and Christian Smith. 2001. *Divided by Faith: Evangelical Religion and the Problem of Race in America*. New York: Oxford University Press.

Fikri, Kenan, Daniel Newman, and Kennedy O'dell. 2021. "Uplifting America's Left Behind Places: A Roadmap for a More Equitable Economy." https://eig. org/wp-content/uploads/2021/02/Spatial-Inequality-Policy-Brief.pdf.

Flint, R Warren. 2013. *Practice of Sustainable Community Development: A Participatory Framework for Change*. New York: Springer.

Fullilove, Mindy. 2016. *Root Shock: How Tearing up City Neighborhoods Hurts America, and What We Can Do About It*. New York: New Village Press. (Kindle)

"Gentrification Explained | Urban Displacement Project." 2017. Urbandisplacement.Org. 2017. https://www.urbandisplacement.org/gentrification-explained.

Greene, Michael. 2014. *A Way out of No Way: The Economic Prerequisites of the Beloved Community*. Eugene, Oregon: Cascade Books.

Grenz, Stanley J, and William C Placher. 2003. *Essentials of Christian Theology*. Louisville: Westminster John Knox Press.

Hartshorne, Charles, and International Society For Science And Religion. 2007. *Omnipotence and Other Theological Mistakes*. Cambridge: International Society For Science And Religion.

Heifetz, Ronald A, Alexander Grashow, and Martin Linsky. 2009. *The Practice of Adaptive Leadership: Tools and Tactics for Changing Your Organization and the World*. Boston, MA: Harvard Business Press.

Hendricks, Obery M. 2006. *The Politics of Jesus: Rediscovering the True Revolutionary Nature of the Teachings of Jesus and How They Have Been Corrupted*. New York: Doubleday.

Herbert, S (2005) The trapdoor of community. *Annals of the Association of American Geographers* 95(4):850–865

Hill, Craig C. 2016. *Servant of All: Status, Ambition, and the Way of Jesus*. Grand Rapids, Michigan: William B. Eerdmans Publishing Company.

Hobson, Maurice J. 2019. *The Legend of the Black Mecca: Politics and Class in the Making of Modern Atlanta*. Chapel Hill: The University of North Carolina Press.

"How States Can Direct Economic Development to Places and People in Need." n.d. Pew.org. Accessed February 9, 2021. https://www.pewtrusts.org/en/research-and-analysis/reports/2021/02/how-states-can-direct-economic-development-to-places-and-people-in-need.

"Impacts of Gentrification: A Policy Primer." 2016. Wharton Public Policy Initiative. 2016. https://publicpolicy.wharton.upenn.edu/live/news/1581-impacts-of-gentrification-a-policy-primer/for-students/blog/news.php.

Inwood, Joshua F.J. 2009. "Searching for the Promised Land: Examining Dr. Martin Luther King's Concept of the Beloved Community." *Antipode* 41 (3): 487–508. https://doi.org/10.1111/j.1467-8330.2009.00684.x.

Jacobs, Jane, and Jason Epstein. 2011. *The Death and Life of Great American Cities.* New York: Modern Library.

King Jr., Martin Luther. 2010 [originally 1967]. *Where Do We Go from Here: Chaos or Community?* Boston: Beacon Press.

Lang, Clarence. 2009. *Grassroots at the Gateway: Class Politics and Black Freedom Struggle in St. Louis, 1936-75.* Ann Arbor, MI: University of Michigan Press.

Lewis, John. 2020. "Together You Can Redeem the Soul," *New York Times.* July 31, 2020. https://www.nytimes.com/2020/07/30/opinion/john-lewis-civil-rights-america.html.

Lupton, Robert D. 2007. *Compassion, Justice, and the Christian Life: Rethinking Ministry to the Poor.* Ventura, CA: Regal Books.

"Mapping the Legacy of Structural Racism in Philadelphia." n.d. Office of the Controller. https://controller.phila.gov/philadelphia-audits/mapping-the-legacy-of-structural-racism-in-philadelphia

Marable, Manning. 1983. *How Capitalism Underdeveloped Black America.* Boston, MA: South End Pr.

Mckim, Donald K. 1996. *Westminster Dictionary of Theological Terms.* Louisville, KY: Westminster/John Knox Press.

Mckissick, Floyd B. 1969. *Three-Fifths of a Man.* New York: Macmillan.

Meltzer, Graham Stuart. 2005. *Sustainable Community: Learning from the Cohousing Model.* Ireland: Trafford Publishing.

"Memorial Place – Playing with Purpose in Baton Rouge, Louisiana." Well360 Health Impact Study. June 2020.

Mihailo Temali. 2012. *The Community Economic Development Handbook: Strategies and Tools to Revitalize Your Neighborhood.* Nashville: Fieldstone Alliance. (Kindle)

"Mission Waco, Mission World ~ Waco, TX." n.d. Missionwaco.org. Accessed February 1, 2021. https://missionwaco.org.

Nelson, Charles R. 2006. *Keynesian Fiscal Policy and the Multipliers.* https://faculty.washington.edu/cnelson/Chap11.pdf

Newport, Gus. 2004. "When Half the Neighborhood Is Missing." *New England Journal of Public Policy:* Vol. 20: Iss.1, Article 21. http://scholarworks.umb.edu/nejpp/vol20/iss1/21.

Pattillo, Mary E. 2007. *Black on the Block: The Politics of Race and Class in the City.* Editorial: University Of Chicago Press.

Qureshi, Zia. 2020. "Tackling the Inequality Pandemic: Is There a Cure?" Brookings. November 17, 2020. https://www.brookings.edu/research/tackling-the-inequality-pandemic-is-there-a-cure/.

Rieger, Joerg. 2001. *God and the Excluded: Visions and Blind Spots in Contemporary Theology.* Minneapolis: Fortress Press.

Rochester, Shawn D. 2017. *The Black Tax: The Cost of Being Black in America and What You Can Do to Help Create the 6 Million Jobs and 1.4 Million Businesses That Are Missing in the Black Community.* Southbury, CT: Good Steward Publishing.

Scheffler, Eben. 2013. "Poverty Eradication and the Bible in Context: A Serious Challenge." *Studia Historiae Ecclesiasticae* 39 (August): 129–153. http://www.scielo.org.za/scielo.php?script=sci_arttext&pid=S1017-04992013000300009.

Sengupta, Gunja. 2009. *From Slavery to Poverty: The Racial Origins of Welfare in New York, 1840-1918.* New York: New York University Press, Cop.

Shipler, David K. 2009. *The Working Poor: Invisible in America*. Bridgewater, NJ: Baker & Taylor. (Kindle)

Staheli L (2008) Citizenship and the Problem of Community.

Thurman, Howard. 1996. *Jesus and the Disinherited*. Boston, MA: Beacon Press.

Walker, Theodore. 1992. *Empower the People: Social Ethics for the African-American Church*. Maryknoll, NY: Orbis Books.

Walker, Theodore. 2004. *Mothership Connections: A Black Atlantic Synthesis of Neoclassical Metaphysics and Black Theology (SUNY Series in Constructive Postmodern Thought)*. New York: State University of New York Press.

Walker, Theodore. 2014. "God and Creation." Lecture, Perkins School of Theology, Southern Methodist University.

Walker, Theodore, "A Martin Luther King Jr. Amendment to the U.S. Constitution: Toward the Abolition of Poverty" (2018). Perkins Faculty Research and Special Events. 14. https://scholar.smu.edu/theology_research/14

Walljasper, Jay. 1997. Review of *When Activists Win: The Renaissance of Dudley St. The Nation*, March 3, 1997.

"What Is the Current Poverty Rate in the United States? - UC Davis Center for Poverty Research." 2012. UC Davis Center for Poverty Research. September 12, 2012. https://poverty.ucdavis.edu/faq/what-current-poverty-rate-united-states.